how to survive working ir

Catholic Parish

*A guide for priests,
volunteers and paid parish workers*

CONTENTS

DEDICATION

In memory of Diana's mother,
Joyce Malley (1921–2015)

and

Bernard's father,
Denis Cotter (1917–2015)
who introduced
Diana and Bernard to God
and to parish life for the first time

FOREWORD

In his recent encyclical, Pope Francis describes the parish as

the presence of the Church in a given territory, an environment for hearing God's word, for growth in the Christian life, for dialogue, proclamation, charitable outreach, worship and celebration. In all its activities the parish encourages and trains its members to be evangelisers. It is a community of communities, a sanctuary where the thirsty come to drink in the midst of their journey, and a centre of constant missionary outreach.

Evangelii Gaudium, 28

The parish is the place where most Catholics experience the Church. Here we encounter Christ, who is truly present with us in several ways: in the gathering of the faithful, in the priest who presides, in the Eucharist we receive. Christ is present, too, as we listen to him speaking to us in the Scriptures and through the dedicated witness of so many of our fellow parishioners.

I enthusiastically welcome *How to survive working in a Catholic Parish.* By helping its readers to understand how to survive (and thereby thrive) as they work in their parishes, I hope this book will help clergy and laypeople, paid workers and volunteers to understand their role in the parish and in the Church.

I pray, too, that you will always be close to the people you serve and those you accompany, empowering and encouraging them to use their gifts for the greater good of the community – reaching out to those in the community who are most in need, to those more distant from the Christian community within the world.

Whatever your reason for reading this book, I pray that God will bless you and grant you and those close to you many blessings.

Yours devotedly in Christ

✠ Bernard Longley
Archbishop of Birmingham

A PRIEST'S STORY

by Fr Bernard Cotter

Imagine a juggler. If he is fairly competent, he can juggle three balls easily. He can complete other tasks at the same time – talking, smiling, singing, maybe even, if he is a super-juggler, riding a unicycle. Another ball is thrown at random; sometimes he can incorporate it, sometimes not. I am that juggler.

Juggling is the story of a priest in a parish. Three or four things happen most days, often simultaneously: daily Mass is celebrated, people are sick and need pastoral care, meetings are planned and schools look for attention. Add to these the callers to the door or on the phone, who often demand instant answers at inopportune moments. Then the juggler receives another ball at random – a missive from the bishop's office, an unexpected child-safeguarding issue in a parish facility, or a funeral suddenly arranged to coincide or even clash with another liturgy already scheduled for the same church on the same day. These random other balls can be incorporated sometimes – or can ruin the whole day or month. This is my life.

Parish ministry is wonderful, as long as you're fairly resilient. It's full of surprises, with endless variety. On my first Saturday in a suburban parish in Cork after I was ordained in 1984, I celebrated a baptism, presided over the reception of remains, heard confessions, led a Vigil Mass and gave benediction after a "holy half-hour". At the time, I thought it was an extraordinary coincidence of events; now I see that it's closer to the norm than I realised then. Thirty-one years on and six parishes later (suburban, commuter-belt, inner-city, American and rural Irish), it seems almost a calm day in a parish.

I have had days in parish life when a funeral, marriage and baptism were celebrated in rapid succession. I am also aware of a parish in my Diocese of Cork & Ross with just two priests, where four funeral masses were celebrated one Christmas Eve (one of them very tragic), interspersed with Christmas confessions and followed by two Christmas masses after sunset. Parish life demands extraordinary resilience and patience.

John O'Donoghue, the Irish spiritual writer and one-time Galway priest, summed up parish life in one word: relentless. The word suits, because parishes are alive 365 days a year. You spend days and weeks planning a major parish event only to find a funeral turns up on the same day and some irreplaceable person, intimately involved with the project, is unexpectedly taken ill. And yet God's show must go on: parish ministers adapt or sink. Variety is indeed the spice of life, certainly of parish life.

If a priest in a parish doesn't pray, his spiritual battery won't take him very far, but the truth is, sometimes there just isn't time. That's the nature of parish life and the adaptability and availability required of the parish minister. The other secret is rest and recreation: days off, holidays, time to reflect, time to write books like this.

How to survive working in a Catholic parish? I am still trying to find out the answer. Maybe in another twenty years I will have cracked it. I certainly wish a book like this was thrust into my newly anointed hands as I started work at my first parish.

A LAYPERSON'S STORY

by Diana Klein

I worked part-time in a parish as a catechetical coordinator while I was studying theology. One of my responsibilities was to help to lead the Liturgy of the Word with children at Sunday Mass. There were lots of children in the parish, so we divided them into two groups: pre-First Communion and post-First Communion. I took my place on the rota; but I also prepared a liturgy for each Sunday in case one of the other leaders didn't show up.

One Saturday night, I had a dinner party and people didn't leave until very late. I hadn't prepared anything for the morning, so I took a quick look at the readings of the day and checked my resource books to get some ideas. It was one of those years when the feast of Ss Peter and Paul fell on a Sunday – and lo and behold, my books didn't offer any help for when that feast replaced the ordinary Sunday readings. I said a quick prayer, hoping that the other catechists would be there in the morning, and went to bed.

Not surprisingly, I woke up late in the morning and rushed to the parish, only to learn that neither of the other leaders had arrived. The priest told me that we'd have to combine the two age groups into one and that I could just adapt whatever I'd prepared. He was about to begin Mass and seemed annoyed that I was running late, so I didn't have the nerve to tell him I hadn't prepared anything! I went into the church and prayed for inspiration on how I might break open the Gospel. I was, at that point, a third-year student of theology; but still, I was completely blank on what I could tell the children about Ss Peter and Paul.

It was only when one of the catechists closed the lectionary after reading the Gospel that I got an idea. I didn't know the younger children well so I introduced myself, explaining that I came from New York with my job and met an Englishman, got married and stayed in London. Children love to hear your stories; I had them in the palm of my hand as I told them mine. I nearly cried at the loving way they responded.

I was very close to my father, even though he lived in New York; and I missed him a lot. When I became pregnant, my father would call me every Sunday afternoon to see how I was. The baby was due in December and my father hoped that the baby would arrive on his birthday. After Nicholas was born, my father said he would come to visit in the spring; but, sadly, he died just two weeks before he was expected to arrive so he never met his grandson.

I went on to tell the children that when Nicholas was about five years old, something happened that upset

me. Nicholas said, "If your dad was here, he would say, 'Be happy'," and he hugged me. I was amazed; that is exactly what my father would have said! I had a photo of my dad on the piano and I used to tell Nicholas stories about what he and I did when I was a child – and about how we would go for long walks together and talk for hours. Nicholas knew my father even though he had never met him. This was just like the story of St Paul, who hadn't met Jesus in person either. He and St Peter both loved Jesus and wanted everyone to know him, to share their experiences of him and to show how much God loves us all.

How to survive working in a Catholic parish as a layperson? Don't ever forget the power of prayer!

INTRODUCTION

*H*ow to survive working in a Catholic Parish is for anyone who does voluntary work in a parish, anyone who is an employee or an employer in a parish – and anyone who is thinking about working in one. It is designed to answer some of your questions (perhaps, even ones you don't know you have) and to allay some of your anxieties and concerns.

Is this book just for laypeople?

Definitely not! Newly ordained deacons and priests, priests recently appointed to a parish, Catholics (non-practising and practising), seminarians and Religious and even non-Catholics will all have questions about parish life. For example, you might be asked to arrange a funeral in a Catholic church but you aren't sure of the order of things. Your help might be sought by a couple getting married who wonder what readings to pick for their marriage. In these and many other dilemmas, this book will help you, but it's actually for *everyone* who is part of a Catholic parish. Most of us are not experts; none of us knows everything. A sign of intelligence is being aware of the questions you need to ask. So, don't be afraid to admit you don't know, that you have questions and concerns, or that you sometimes ask yourself (as we all do), "What on earth am I doing here?"

The book aims to be real and to deal with issues in a down-to-earth way. We have been careful to use "non-churchy" language – especially when we refer to Church teaching and Canon Law. The theology underlying the book will be what we call "applied" or "practical" theology. Practical theology attempts to deal with issues that are part of life in the world. It doesn't try to discuss or solve abstract theories. Think of this book as a practical guide to surviving (and we hope thriving!) in a Catholic parish.

Is this book just for the people who do the "holy" stuff?

Again, absolutely not! The book is designed for a wide variety of readers, who between them will have a broad range of knowledge and experience of all things Catholic. It is for everyone who works in a Catholic parish – volunteers, parish secretaries or administrators, cleaners or caretakers and those who are involved in pastoral ministry.

Please read this book in whatever way it suits you. If you are a volunteer, for example, or if you are looking for volunteers to help in some parish work, you will find Chapter 3 of special interest. If you are considering applying for a job in a parish or if you are looking to employ a layperson in the parish, Chapter 4 is essential reading. If you have been asked to prepare the liturgy for a special Mass, you will find Chapter 5 helpful; it will help you navigate your way around the Church year and some of the rites and rituals. And, if you don't understand a word or an expression, check out the glossary of terms in Appendix II.

Take time to think and reflect

Throughout the book, we have shared good practice from parishes we know. We've drawn upon articles giving concrete examples of how to be a welcoming parish with good liturgies, meaningful preaching and catechesis. We've also included a space at the end of every chapter for reflection and prayer. We hope that this book will be relevant to you and your life, and will reassure you that your role in the parish is meaningful.

Be assured, too, that God reveals himself in different ways. As St Paul wrote in his letter to the Romans, God shows his power and nature through his created world (Romans 2). God's moral nature is seen in our conscience; all people have a sense of right and wrong. But, most of all, God reveals himself through Christ, who uses human events and words to communicate with us. God's guiding presence reassures us when we are anxious about what we are doing or how we are going about it.

Diana Klein   *Bernard Cotter*

A note about Vatican and other Church documents

We have used quotes from Church documents. Sometimes the titles are in Latin; but don't let that put you off. If you want to read further, you will find most of them translated into accessible English on the Vatican website: www.vatican.va.
In Appendix III, we have included a list of these documents as well as the books we've referenced and a list of useful websites.

A note about articles from The Tablet

We also share ideas first floated in the Parish Practice page of *The Tablet*; you'll see in the endnotes which articles were most helpful to us. The endnotes include information about the articles we have drawn from; and, even if you are not a subscriber, you can access the full articles on *The Tablet* website, www.tablet.co.uk by selecting "archive" then "browse all issues" where you will find the issue containing the article.

CHAPTER 1

THE PARISH: *Is it an area or a community?*

The word parish has always referred to an area of territory, but the purpose of the organisation of that area has varied. There were times in the Catholic Church's history when a parish was seen as the right size of area to provide an income for a priest.

The Code of Canon Law of 1983, however, clarified that parishes were primarily for the benefit of the faithful rather than the priest, defining a parish as a community of Christ's faithful within a particular church (diocese), whose pastoral care is entrusted to a parish priest as its proper pastor (Canon 515 §1). In addition, there is provision that, as a general rule, a parish is to be territorial, that is, it is to embrace all Christ's faithful of a given territory. While all of Christ's faithful are embraced and welcomed in their local church, some parishes, however, insist that they take the first step by registering as members of the parish.

Jesus' first followers formed a community

Parishes have always been communities. Most of the first followers of Jesus were pious Jews in a Jewish culture who apparently kept the Sabbath according to contemporary Jewish customs. They attended Jewish festivals and observed Temple rituals, as described in the Acts of the Apostles. They went as a body to the Temple every day but met on the Sabbath to share a meal and to break bread in their houses which were the focus of early Christian worship (see Acts 2:46). Their meals had an important religious theme; having a meal together, praising God and praying together, they believed, increased the unity among those present (Acts 2:47).

By the very nature of meeting in homes, these congregations were not large; each assembly was only as large as the biggest room in a given home. Gradually, as numbers increased, and for practical reasons, the communal meals disappeared, although the breaking of the bread continued to be their focus. Special buildings called *basilicoi* (basilicas) were needed to accommodate this growing number; the celebrations were transferred from the Jewish Sabbath to Sunday, the first day of the week – since that was the day that Jesus rose from the dead.

The Eucharist soon became the normal way of celebrating the Lord's Day and bringing Christians together on Sundays in what became their parishes. St Paul stresses the variety of roles and activities of its leaders and members in those early days of the Church. We read in 1 Corinthians that, in the early Christian community, not all the members have the same function. The community was served by a variety of spiritual gifts and activities, including the speaking of wisdom, knowledge, faith, gifts of healing, working of miracles, prophecy, discernment of spirits, various kinds of tongues, and interpretation of tongues (1 Corinthians 12:4-10). Similarly, we read in Paul's letter to the Romans that our gifts differ according to the grace given to us: "prophecy, in proportion to faith; ministry, in ministering; the teacher, in teaching; the exhorter, in exhortation; the giver, in generosity; the leader, in diligence; the compassionate, in cheerfulness" (Romans 12:6-8).

Parishes vary from Church to Church

Christians of many hues arrange themselves in local organisations. The Roman Catholic, Orthodox, Anglican and Church of Scotland call them parishes; the Methodist Church calls them congregations or circuits. These are administrative units under the care of a pastor or priest, and operate within a larger church body. The term "parish" came from the Latin word *parocoeia*, a Latinised version of the Greek word παροικία, which originally referred to neighbours or people staying near each other. This original sense of parish denoting people persists; today the term refers to the people living within an administrative unit as well as to the unit itself. When people speak of loyalty to their parish, this loyalty is meant to apply equally to the local area and to the people living within it.

The relationship between the parish and the diocese varies. In the Church of Ireland, and in the Scottish Episcopal Church and in the American Anglican province, more power appears to be delegated to the parish via the local vestries, which consist of a gathering of local parishioners or their representatives, empowered to make decisions for the parish. In the Church of England, the parochial church councils have a similar role and are involved in the selection of clergy for the parish.

For a Catholic parish, on the other hand, communion with the local diocese and its bishop is very important and must always be maintained, as well as its operation within the teaching of the Church (which is similar to the Orthodox in this regard). Parishioners or clergy who transfer from one Church to another need to become aware of the fundamental differences in how parishes are organised and empowered from Church to Church.

The Church is more than a hierarchy

Like any community, the Church organises itself into roles, and this chapter features some of the people who make up the parish of today, and the roles they play – and the activities of its leaders and members. We will look at some of the important principles adopted by the Second Vatican Council which are embodied in its teaching that the Church is the "People of God".

The Dogmatic Constitution on the Church (*Lumen Gentium*) presented the fullest, most detailed understanding of the Church ever developed by a Council. The practical application of this theology is offered in five decrees which consider different groups within the People of God: the laity, the bishops, priests (and their formation) and the religious life.

In *Lumen Gentium,* the Church tells us that first and foremost we are the people, gathered under Christ, the head of the Church (LG 33). While it is an institution, it continues primarily to be a community.

Chapter 3 is on the hierarchy of the Church; it attempts to clarify how all the People of God fulfil our mission in history. It begins by saying that Christ instituted various forms of ministry, directed for the benefit of all. In other words, the Church is not only the hierarchy, the clergy and members of religious communities, but the whole community of the baptised. In fact, everything that the Council has said about the People of God applies to all the members – lay, religious and clerical. The Church's mission to the world is to be undertaken by all the faithful.

As scripture tells us, all the members of the Church form one body (Romans 12:4-5); we are all one in Christ (Galatians 3:28). The fact is that everyone in the Church is called to holiness and to the fullness of the Christian life, which is conducive to a more human way of living in faith, hope and love.

The laity

The overwhelming majority of Catholics are laypeople. The word lay derives from the Anglo-French *lai* which derives from the Late Latin *laicus*; from the Greek λαϊκός – *laikos*: of the people, from λαός – *laos*: the people at large.

There are two Vatican II documents in particular devoted to the apostolate of the laity: *Apostolicam Actuositatem* and the fourth chapter of *Lumen Gentium*. The term "laity" includes the faithful except those in holy orders.

These faithful are by baptism made one body with Christ and are constituted among the People of God; they are in their own way made sharers in the priestly, prophetical, and kingly functions of Christ; and they carry out for their own part the mission of the whole Christian people in the Church and in the world.

Lumen Gentium, 31

Members of religious orders

A member of a religious order is often simply referred to as a "Religious". The terms "monk" and "nun" refer to members of enclosed religious orders, while members of orders which are not enclosed are usually referred to as religious sisters or religious brothers (or religious priests). A "novice" is someone who has been accepted into a religious order and who is undergoing a period of training and formation (or "novitiate") before taking any vows. Typically, these vows are poverty, chastity and obedience. Except for those called to be hermits, Religious live in community. With variations that allow for an abundance of charisms and works of the Spirit, religious orders follow three paths:

- **Contemplative:** whose main vocation is to pray for the world. They live in religious houses or monasteries and in some cases never leave. You could describe them as the great prayer powerhouses of the Church.

- **Monastic:** who also live in monasteries. Their calling involves greater interaction with the world than contemplatives. They often run schools or run houses to care for the poor, elderly, sick or dying. Sometimes monastic orders serve a parish community and that parish functions as other parishes, with a defined parish priest who may be one of the priests of the monastic community. Just as a parish priest serves the parish community so in such cases do monastic orders; the parish they serve is no more and no less than a parish.

- **Apostolic:** meaning they are founded to work in the world and, although they have a very clear commitment to a life of prayer, their key function is to serve God through caring for others and taking the Gospel to places where it is not known or to which there is (in some cases great) hostility. Religious called to the apostolic path are to be found in many parts of the world and in many different work-roles. Some sisters work as pastoral assistants in parishes as part of their apostolic work. Some communities of Religious priests can take responsibility for a parish as part of their apostolic outreach.

Deacons, Priests, Bishops

Holy orders is the sacrament of apostolic ministry. It includes three degrees: diaconate, presbyterate and episcopate.

Deacons

Deacons are ordained to serve at the altar and in the community. Deacons assist at the altar during Mass and preach God's word in the homily. In addition, they preside at baptisms, marriages and funerals. They also have a role in the community – encouraging the social caring ministry of the parish as a whole.

There are two kinds of deacons. One is the "transitional" deacon – someone who has been ordained as a deacon as the final stage of preparation to be ordained as a priest and who normally remains a deacon for about a year. The other type is the "permanent" deacon, ordained by the bishop to that role and who will remain a deacon. Permanent deacons are often older married men and they will not go on to be ordained as priests. They can do much in the parish; but they cannot celebrate Mass or the sacrament of reconciliation or the sacrament of anointing.

Priests

When considering the role of a priest, we cannot just outline the things he does; it is *who he is* that matters first and foremost. A priest first of all is a baptised man who has heard God calling him to a particular role in the Church – that of ministerial priesthood. He should be a man who cares about people and celebrates with them, commiserates with them and offers help and advice when it's needed.

Through the ordained ministry of bishops and priests, the presence of Christ is made visible in the midst of the community of believers. They act in the name of the whole Church – which does not mean that they are the delegates of the community. It is because the ministerial priesthood represents Christ that it can represent the Church.

Priests have many different roles in parish life. The leader of the parish is the parish priest (called the "pastor" in the US). Priests are collaborators with the diocesan bishops in the work of evangelisation and catechesis; their primary responsibility is preaching the Gospel. They must also promote the responsibility of all Christians to transmit the faith, by adequate preaching, by close contact with them so as to invite them to play their part in the fundamental task of evangelisation.

In parishes with more than one priest, the other priests often have different roles that may need clarification.

Traditionally, parishes had curates or assistant priests whose role was to help the parish priest carry out his role. Retired priests may live locally and help out in the parish's liturgy (as may priests whose primary job is elsewhere, e.g. in the marriage tribunal or in teaching) but they would have no direct role in parish life and no voice on the parish team. Part of the challenge of anyone hoping to survive working in a Catholic parish is to ensure the roles and responsibilities of all the priests in the parish are clear.

Most priests in parishes are "secular" priests, i.e. subject to a bishop and part of a particular diocese. However, some religious orders take responsibility for parishes and administer them on behalf of the bishop: these work out of the particular charism of their order but also try to operate within the pastoral plan of the diocese. Priests who are members of societies of secular clergy (often missionary societies) do the same.

So, what's the bishop's job?

The bishop is appointed directly by the Pope. He is responsible for the running of a diocese and has full authority within his own diocese. The Vatican II document that describes the pastoral office of bishops in the Church is *Christus Dominus* (CD). These are the offices of a bishop:

- **The teaching office** and the proclamation of the Gospel occupy the pre-eminent position. The bishops are described as authentic teachers – especially concerned about catechetical instruction and making sure that the catechists are properly prepared for their task.

- **The office of sanctifying** should be understood in connection with the fact that the bishop is the chief presider at the community assembly for the Eucharist; it is he who consecrates the Eucharist or has this done at his direction.

- **Ruler (or leader)** – as ruler or leader the bishop should be with his people as one who serves, as a good shepherd who knows his sheep and whose sheep know him, as a true father who excels in his love and solicitude for all. He should unite and mould his flock into one family that all, conscious of their duties, may live and act in the communion of charity.

A bishop should be solicitous for the welfare of his priests – being compassionate and helpful to those who are ill or in any kind of danger, or who have failed in some respect. He must provide for the faithful as their individual circumstances demand and should try to keep himself informed of their needs in the social circumstances in which they live.

He should ensure that the faithful are involved in Church affairs; he should recognise their right and duty to play their part in building up the Mystical Body of Christ – promoting their apostolate according to their state of life and aptitudes. This will, of course, include the fostering of vocations. The important point here is that he must coordinate *all* the gifts and abilities of the people, putting them to good use for the building up of the Church.

Other diocesan bodies help the bishop and support parishes

Most dioceses organise central groupings that provide resources to parishes as well as assisting the bishop in his coordinating role. A director and/or office for pastoral planning usually oversees the development of parishes, particularly in the context of changes in the number of available clergy. Liturgy commissions provide resources to local parish liturgy groups, as do Justice and Peace commissions and social outreach bodies. The diocesan finance officer can advise parish priests on the formation of parish finance committees, a canon law requirement for parishes. Many dioceses also have an office of evangelisation, which will have responsibility for catechesis: adult formation and sacramental preparation.

In every diocese there is a cathedral church, from which the bishop presides over the diocese. To help the bishop in running the cathedral and administering the diocese, almost every cathedral has a group of priests appointed by him to form the "chapter" – or governing body – of the cathedral. Bishops or canons are often responsible for education, or finances, or a particular area of pastoral responsibility. In some cases, "canon" is simply an honorary title, which does not involve belonging to the chapter. In most chapters, officers of the body have specific titles, which may include a dean or provost (the president of the chapter), precentor, chancellor, treasurer, archdeacon and secretary.

In some dioceses, the canons are also given the role of the college of consultors, whom the bishop consults when making diocesan appointments and who appoint the diocesan administrator if the diocese is left without a bishop.

Every diocese also has a council of priests, who help the bishop in the governance of the diocese and he is bound to consult them before making certain serious decisions. This council is to represent the clergy of the diocese, who are entitled to vote representatives onto it. Some of its members may form the college of consultors, if this role has not been assigned to the chapter.

The Code of Canon Law also allows for the establishment of a pastoral council in each diocese, where clerics, religious and laypeople together examine the pastoral works of the diocese and propose practical conclusions.

What's a vicar general?

The vicar general (VG) is a priest appointed to assist in the running of the diocese: he is seen as "second-in-command" to the bishop: larger dioceses will usually have more than one. VGs often have many responsibilities delegated to them by the bishop, so people who work in parishes may well meet them. Although a vicar general will usually be a monsignor by virtue of his office, not all monsignors are vicars general.

 POINTS TO REMEMBER

☑ Catholic parishes are in communion with the local diocese and its bishop and this communion must always be maintained.

☑ Catholic parishes are in communion with the whole Church and operate within the teaching of the Church.

☑ The Church is more than a hierarchy or a territory; it is primarily a community.

POINTS FOR PERSONAL REFLECTION
OR GROUP DISCUSSION

⚠ What is the relationship between your local bishop and your parish?

⚠ In what ways are you aware of belonging to a Church much bigger than your parish which operates within the teaching of the Church?

⚠ When you think of "the Church", do you think of the hierarchy or the local community?

What's a vicar forane?

As well as belonging to a diocese, parishes are grouped together in deaneries, of which there are several in each diocese; these are presided over by a leader appointed by the bishop. This priest may be titled a vicar forane and may convene meetings of priests or staff at the parishes in his deanery. He may be given other roles by the bishop, from a selection included in the Code of Canon Law.

Prayer

God our Father, you gather your people in communities and teach them to love each other: help us always to take a full and active part in our local parish, sharing our gifts and talents, that your glory may be praised and your Kingdom come in our midst. Through Jesus Christ our Lord. Amen.

Other dignitaries: archbishops and cardinals

The archbishop has the same authority as the bishop. He is responsible for a large or important diocese known as an "archdiocese". Cardinals are personally appointed by the Pope. Their primary job is to elect the next pope. However, because the Catholic Church has over a billion members, the Pope relies on around 120 of his cardinals to help run the Church. Some are stationed in Rome, heading up the departments of the Church. This group is called the Roman Curia. Those not based in Rome lead archdioceses around the world and thus have full administrative authority within their areas, like other bishops.

CHAPTER 2

MINISTRY: *To be a Christian is to be a minister*

The Second Vatican Council sought to reinstate the notion of ministry as service rather than an ecclesiastical status. Ministry is no longer a word to be applied only to the ordained – and, as it says in *Lumen Gentium,* there are "a variety of ministries" in the Church (LG 18). In the post-Vatican II Church, many laypeople are now included who were, at one time, excluded from meaningful participation in the liturgical, educational, administrative and social ministries of the Church.

In the last chapter, we said that all baptised people are sharers in the priestly, prophetical and kingly functions of Christ (LG 31). That means that the Church is saying that each of us – committed or not, ordained or not – is empowered by God to do good for others, to render unselfish service to our neighbours. This has led to an expanded understanding of who ministers are and what ministry is.

Ministry in the Church

Every level of ministry is oriented to the same reality – namely, the coming Kingdom of God, a kingdom not only of holiness and grace, but of justice, love and peace. Ministers serve this kingdom in four ways.

First, they are sent to proclaim the Kingdom of God by *word,* that is, in preaching, teaching and catechesis; this work is carried out primarily by priests and catechists.

Secondly, ministers participate in Christ's *worship* of the Father, in and through the power of the Holy Spirit; the various ministers involved in preparing and serving the liturgy are involved here.

Thirdly, ministers offer *witness* to the world by answering the call to justice and peace, challenging global poverty and responding to ecological challenges.

Finally, ministers are sent to provide *service* to those in need – both inside and outside the Church. They do this by following the example of Christ, who ministered to the sick, the poor, the handicapped, the oppressed, the socially ostracised, the sinners and the dying.

Ministry is exercised, therefore, across the whole missionary spectrum.

Ministries of the Word
(in preaching, teaching and catechesis)

Priests and catechists are ministers of the Word, but in different senses. Priests face one of their greatest challenges in writing a homily that is relevant and insightful every week. People come to Mass on Sunday looking for hope and guidance. So the bottom-line question priests have to ask about every homily should always be: "Where is the Good News here?" This question also underlies homilies at baptisms, weddings and funerals.

Catechists proclaim the Kingdom of God by word, whether they serve in the classroom or in the Church. The word "catechesis" comes from the Greek – *kata* meaning "down" and *echein* meaning "to sound". We translate this as "to echo": catechists echo the word of God. Pope St John Paul II wrote a Church document on catechesis titled *Catechesi Tradendae* (On Catechesis in Our Time). In it, he defines catechesis as

> *the whole of the efforts within the Church to make disciples, to help people to believe that Jesus is the Son of God, so that believing they might have life in His name, and to educate and instruct them in this life and thus build up the Body of Christ.* (CT 1)

> *the definitive aim of catechesis is to put people not only in touch but in communion, in intimacy, with Jesus Christ: only He can lead us to the love of the Father in the Spirit and make us share in the life of the Holy Trinity.* (CT 5)

So if you are listening, reading, or seeing something or someone that brings you to a deeper understanding of the Catholic faith and therefore a greater intimacy with Jesus Christ, then you are being catechised. You don't "grow out of" the need for catechesis just like you don't "grow out of" falling deeper in love with your spouse.

Ministries of worship
(liturgical ministries)

Good liturgy draws people together and transforms them into an assembly of worshippers. It is through the variety of liturgical ministries in the Church that the body of Christ is built up:

The priest leads the people in prayer when he presides at Mass in listening and responding to God's word, and in offering the sacrifice through Christ in the Spirit to the Father. He proclaims the message of salvation in preaching and gives the Bread of eternal Life and the Cup of salvation.

The deacon proclaims the Gospel reading at Mass and he may sometimes give the homily. His role is to assist the priest at the chair and at the altar and gives certain directions and invitations to the assembly, especially regarding movement or posture. He also assists in the distribution of Communion to the people.

Readers (ministers of the Word) proclaim the word of God from scripture. They can make a difference to the way people hear the scripture by their conviction, their preparation, and their delivery. If possible, it is better to have a different reader for each reading. The responsorial psalm should ideally be a sung response to the first reading; but, if necessary, may be read by a reader.

Ministers of music (psalmists, cantors, organists and other instrumentalists, choirs, and directors of music) enhance the assembly's full participation in singing the songs, responses, and acclamations. The choir is part of the assembly – serving it by leading it in sung prayer; but it should never displace, or dominate the song of the assembly. The director of music, working collaboratively with other ministers, has responsibility for selecting appropriate musical settings.

Extraordinary ministers of Holy Communion will frequently be needed in distributing Communion if a large number of people are at Mass so that the Communion rite is not unduly long. They will regularly be needed when Communion is given under both kinds, the form of Communion in which the Eucharistic banquet is more clearly signified. It is important to remember that bishops, priests and deacons are the ordinary ministers of Holy Communion and the extraordinary ministers should only serve when there are not enough ordinary ones. They also serve the community by taking Communion to those who are prevented by sickness, old age, or other cause from taking part in the gathering for Mass.

Altar servers exercise their ministry within the assembly and enhance the quality of celebration for the whole assembly by taking part in processions, by ringing the bell and by ensuring that all requisites for the celebration are available at the appropriate moments.

Ushers (also called ministers of welcome or "welcomers") exercise their ministry by greeting people at the church door, making sure they are provided with all necessary books, music, and other items for the celebration, such as candles or palms and helping them find their places.

Sacristans have responsibility for the careful arranging of the liturgical books, the vestments, and other things needed for the celebration of Mass.

Liturgical environment ministers make sure the liturgical space reflects the time of year as well as the liturgical season. Autumnal themes underlie harvest thanksgiving displays, while there is a winter feel to the church when it honours the dead in November. These ministers see to it that the church reflects Advent as well as Christmas, Lent as well as Easter and Pentecost. They are helped by those who provide and arrange flowers and by the others who make sure that the church is kept clean and tidy, fit for its purpose.

Ministries of witness
(helping us live what we proclaim)

Christians witness to the world by responding to the global issues facing humanity. Ministers of witness try to figure out what can be done about racism, economic justice, sexism and environmental degradation, locally as well as globally.

Many dioceses have a commission for **Justice and Peace**, which will support the laity, religious, priests and bishops of the dioceses in developing awareness of, and ensuring engagement with, justice and peace as an integral part of the life of the Church and its living out of Gospel/Kingdom values. Parishes sometimes organise petitions about ethical issues, such as the protection of the unborn child and assisted suicide; they also sign statements against the use of nuclear weapons or war; they make collections of money when disasters strike and they contribute food, money, clothing and other essential items for the poor, for political asylum seekers and refugees. In addition, bidding prayers include pressing matters of the day for local and international issues.

Aid agencies reflect the social mission and core values of the Catholic Church. They serve the world's most vulnerable people across the world, bringing hope and compassion to poor communities, standing side by side with them to end poverty and injustice; they resource ministries of witness at parish level. **Cafod** is the official aid agency of the Catholic Church in England and Wales; **Trócaire** is the Irish equivalent; and **SCIAF** is the official aid agency of the Catholic Church in Scotland.

***Laudato Si'* – the parish's concern for the environment** is core to Catholic theology and activity. In his recent encyclical, *Laudato Si'* (On Care for Our Common Home), Pope Francis challenges parishes, saying he would like us to enter into dialogue with all people about caring for our common home.

Ministries of service
(inside and outside the Church)

The Church sends ministers to provide *service* to those in need – both inside and outside the Church. This follows the example of Christ, who ministered to the sick, the poor, the handicapped, the oppressed, the socially ostracised, the sinners and the dying. Here are some examples of this ministry:

Parish-life coordinators
According to Canon Law, a diocesan bishop can entrust a share in the pastoral care of a parish to a qualified person other than a priest in times of clergy shortage (Canon 517.2). Different titles are used for this role, including parish director and pastoral administrator; the most commonly used term in the US is parish-life coordinator. When this happens, the

bishop will appoint a canonical pastor, a priest who will have responsibility for the general oversight of the parish – although he is not physically present or involved in day-to-day activities. The parish-life coordinator is the one who is pastorally present and responsible for parish administration, with one or more visiting priests assisting the parish with sacramental needs.[1]

Ministers to the youth

Youth ministry is much more than youth groups, service projects, retreats and events. It involves facilitating a comprehensive service that integrates young people into the life, mission and work of the Catholic faith-community as disciples of Jesus Christ. It encompasses volunteer recruitment, training and management; leadership development for youth and adults; faith formation; expertise in prayer and worship, and much more.

Ministers to the elderly

Parishes minister to the elderly in many ways, including the facilitation of Friendship Clubs and other social groupings, and by seasonal events like Christmas dinners and summer outings. A formal grouping like Ascent may assist your parish as you seek to broaden the ministry to the elderly.

Ascent is a movement of elderly and middle-aged men and women whose children are now grown up and/or who, more or less, have come to the end of their professional careers or their salary or wage earning activities. Members meet at regular intervals in the parish centre. Meetings begin with refreshments, followed by a short prayer and the study of a Gospel passage or other Church document.

Members exchange views on what they have studied and then try and see how their study, discussion and personal experience can help them to put into practice their individual and collective Christian mission. This movement exists in five continents, in some forty countries where it carries different names, e.g. Vie Montante, Vida Ascendente, Life Ascending and Ascending Life (www.ascentmovement.org.uk).

Ministers to the sick

Priests, pastoral workers and extraordinary ministers of Holy Communion can offer a valuable service to the elderly, those who are sick and physically immobile in our parishes by visiting them at home or in nursing homes and bringing them Holy Communion. Remember, they are still part of the parish – and loneliness and isolation is a serious problem.

These ministers must be sensitive and intuitive individuals who know when to visit and how long to stay – and their agenda must always concentrate on those they are visiting. In some parishes, the ministers bring the parish bulletin when they visit so that the housebound and those parishioners who are in nursing homes are kept up to date with what is happening in the parish. They might be asked to pray for people preparing for the sacraments and for those in some kind of difficulty – be it financial, marital or any other kind of problem.[2]

Parishes should remind people regularly to register their religion if they are admitted to hospital confirming that this information may be passed to the Spiritual and Pastoral Care Department of the hospital. Few people look forward to a stay in hospital, but if it becomes necessary, it is important

that they are well cared for – and that includes providing for spiritual, pastoral and religious needs. Chaplains offer a friendly face, a listening ear, a chance to share thoughts and concerns as well as prayer, religious and sacramental care. They can provide support in coping with illness, bereavement, caring for others, workplace problems – or simply when you need someone to talk to.

Hospitals can be very lonely and frightening places for even the most confident adults. To help alleviate these stresses some parishes train and commission "hospital visitor teams", to accompany parishioners and maintain a link between them and the praying community. These ensure that the sick are often remembered in the Prayer of the Faithful at Sunday Mass.

It's also vital that children who need a stay in hospital do not feel alone and abandoned. Inspired by how some hospital chaplains support and encourage children through what is often a difficult time, Fr Peter Scott has put together a hospital prayer-and-activities book: its aim is to help every child in hospital grow closer to Jesus and to become aware that he is always with and near each one of them. The book offers ideas for prayers for the child's family, the doctors and nurses looking after him or her, new patients on the ward and so on. It is the kind of book a parish priest or parish team can keep a supply of to give to children when they are in hospital or when they are preparing to go into hospital.[3]

Ministers to the poor and homeless

Helping the homeless can be fraught with all kinds of difficulties. A young priest in his first parish tells the story of answering the door to the presbytery only to be met with a man placing an order for one cup of tea, one cup of coffee with sugar and two cheese sandwiches without pickle. He closed the door on the man, but he was barely back in his room when the man rang the doorbell again. When he got there, he found the parish priest carrying a tray with the man's lunch order. This process, he said, continued all day; it seemed to him that the work of the parish was centred on the homeless and their need for food from morning till night. When the young priest was asked to take over the running of this service, he appealed in the parish newsletter for volunteers to help run a "tea and sandwich" service four days a week. It involved spending some time in the morning preparing sandwiches and tea and then, for a specific time only, serving it between 1.45 and 2pm. Forty-five people came forward and the project became a thriving community-building ministry. [4]

In recent years, homelessness and poverty have become more commonplace. Many parishes today work in collaboration with other local churches to provide services like this so that the homeless have somewhere to go every day to get something to eat. During the worst of the winter months, they also provide a hot meal, overnight accommodation, company and real advice and guidance to homeless guests. Parishes can, of course, ignore the issue of homelessness on their doorstep; but, as Christians, we do so at our peril. The gains, apart from helping the homeless themselves, include the opportunities of building parish and local community – and offer a truly visible witness to the world that they are followers of Jesus.

Ministry to prisoners and ex-prisoners
One of the world's largest cosmetic companies concluded its advertisements by telling people that they should use their products "because they are worth it". It's a catchy marketing phrase. A prison chaplain told me that he would like to say this to all the people he meets – in prison and those leaving prison – in the hope that they too might be able to recognise their self-worth.

He tells the story of a young man he met in prison who came to every Mass in the prison and to many of the faith-sharing meetings. Clearly, he said, faith and belonging meant a huge amount to him. The day before he was released, he told the chaplain that he would go to Mass every Sunday in his local parish. About two months later, they met again; the man was back in the same prison. He said he had gone to Mass every Sunday for three weeks but nobody spoke to him; and, after Mass, everybody went

away and he felt so very alone.[5] Ask yourself if every stranger who comes to Mass in your parish feels they are part of a welcoming, inclusive family.

Ministry to families
Family ministry is a key ministry of service provided by the Church at parish level. This involves walking with people in a huge variety of complex situations: cohabitation, civil marriage, mixed and interreligious marriages, gay people, people whose marriages have broken down, abandoned spouses, single parents, as well as divorced people who have civilly remarried.

The 2015 Synod on the Family issued a very strong call for the divorced and remarried to be integrated into the life of the Church, so that they do not feel themselves to be excommunicated but "can live and mature as living members of the Church", as its report stated. Preparation and support for marriage is another feature of family ministry, as is the pastoral accompaniment of young couples in the first years of their marriage

Ministry to those with learning disabilities
The members of our community with learning disabilities have a rightful place in the very heart of the Church. Given the growth in understanding of intellectual disabilities and the progress that has been made in specialised pedagogy, we now know that it is possible and desirable for people of all abilities to have adequate catechesis – and this is ratified in the *General Directory for Catechesis* (GDC 189). The wide development of alternative and creative methods of catechesis which do not rely solely on the literate or verbal has had an impact on mainstream catechesis.[6]

Ministry to lapsed Catholics

People who are not practising their faith should, of course, be made to feel welcome if they want to come back to the Church. No one disagrees with that. It is important, though, not to be discouraged when some people don't want to come back – and to remember that, even in the Lord's time, some who heard his teaching fell away (John 6:60. 66).

The best that ministers can offer those who are no longer practising is an invitation to come back and a listening ear as to the reasons why they left in the first place. They may simply have drifted away, they may have been busy with work or young children and fell out of the habit of coming to Mass – or, they may have experienced hurt in the Church. Where this is the case, the lapsed need to come to understand that the whole Church is not to blame, just the ones who hurt them.

If lapsed or inactive Catholics want to practise again, they can do so simply by making a good confession. But Catholics who have been inactive a long time or have issues with the Church may want (or need) a slower re-entry process. There are various programmes available to help Catholics return to the Church which will assist those involved in this ministry, such as *Landings, Catholics Come Home, Keeping in Touch* and *Catholics returning home*. It is the work of the whole parish and part of evangelisation to encourage and nurture the spiritual longings of returning Catholics.

POINTS TO REMEMBER

- ☑ According to *Lumen Gentium*, there are a "variety of ministries" in the Church (LG 18).
- ☑ Every baptised person is gifted and called to ministry.
- ☑ Every level of ministry looks to the coming Kingdom of God, a kingdom not only of holiness and grace, but of justice, love and peace.
- ☑ The mission of the Church is seen in ministries of *word*, *worship*, *witness* and *service*.

POINTS FOR PERSONAL REFLECTION OR GROUP DISCUSSION

- If you were asked to put together an advertising campaign to interest more laypeople in church ministries, how would you go about it?
- Ask yourself if every stranger who comes to Mass in your parish feels they are part of a welcoming and inclusive family.
- Reflect on the imagery of a beautiful Persian rug with its many different colours making its design. Each plays an important part; each one complementing the others – all woven together. Does this image describe your parish, the Church? What image would you use?

Reflection

Christ has no body now on earth but yours; no hands but yours; no feet but yours.
Yours are the eyes through which the compassion of Christ must look out on the world.
Yours are the feet with which he is to go about doing good.
Yours are the hands with which He is to bless His people.

Excerpt from the prayer of
St Teresa of Avila (1515–1582)

ENDNOTES

[1] From a Parish Practice article by Mary Foley, "Into the breach", *The Tablet*, 16 May 2009.

[2] Some of the ideas in this section from a Parish Practice article by Peter Michael Scott, "Out of confinement", *The Tablet*, 6 July 2013.

[3] Some of the ideas in this section from a Parish Practice article by Peter Michael Scott, "Life jacket for children" issue of *The Tablet*, 11 January 2014.

[4] From a Parish Practice article by Dominic McKenna, "Someone is knocking", *The Tablet*, 30 January 2010.

[5] From a Parish Practice article written by Malachy Keegan, "We are not alone", *The Tablet*, 15 November 2008.

[6] From a Parish Practice article by Diana Klein, "When necessary, use words", *The Tablet*, 15 March 2014.

CHAPTER 3

VOLUNTEERS: *Wanted and needed in parish life*

Volunteering can make a real difference to your own life and the lives of those around you; and opportunities to volunteer come in many shapes and sizes. The London Olympics and Paralympics in 2012 demonstrated the impact volunteering can have, if properly resourced, supported and managed. The 70,000 Olympic volunteers who gave their time and energy are believed to be the key to the Games' success. The volunteer programme was underpinned by effective volunteer management and principles of good practice – including recognition – and it offers a good example of how to manage and support volunteers.

Every person in the parish is uniquely gifted to volunteer in the parish and to enable Christ's Church to grow – and every person should feel welcome to offer their gifts. Some volunteer a few hours regularly, others when called upon by the parish.

Like the Olympic volunteers, parish volunteers are key to the successful parish. And, just as bishops, priests and deacons have been given the authority of ordination to exercise leadership as servants of the People of God, so through baptism and confirmation laypeople have been given rights and responsibilities to participate in the mission of the Church.

Are volunteers "Father's helpers" or are they answering a call to mission?

There has been a change of perception in what volunteers are. Volunteers used to be the people who *helped Father out* when he needed something done, i.e. helping with the routine job of cleaning the church or laundering the altar linens. More and more today, volunteers do not see themselves as helping someone else out, but simply "being church" – helping *themselves* out, doing what they do by baptismal right, not just by permission and kindness. In the *Parish of the New Millennium*, William Bausch says they are apt to have a sense of ownership whose larger objective is the overall need and benefit to the parish as a whole. They take the initiative, relying on their personal call and charism and sense of mission without needing the constant approval of the priest.

What do volunteers in the parish do?

There are volunteers doing all kinds of things in the parish, such as:

- **Parish pastoral council** who coordinate the pastoral life of the parish

- **Finance committee** who advise the parish priest on financial matters

- **Liturgy planning group** who prepare the parish's main liturgies

- **Pastoral care ministers** whose role includes visiting the sick in hospital and at home, bereavement visiting or counselling, pastoral care for families and for the separated or divorced

- **Liturgical ministries** that include a variety of roles: extraordinary ministers of Holy Communion (distributing Communion in the church and to the housebound), readers, music ministries (both musicians and choir members), altar servers, sacristans and flower arrangers; assistant presiders at parish funeral liturgies and non-eucharistic weekday liturgies

- **Catechists** who help couples work towards engagement and marriage; they help adults prepare for baptism or to be received into the Catholic Church through the RCIA (Rite of Christian Initiation of Adults); they help parents understand their infant's baptism; they prepare young people for the sacraments of first reconciliation, First Communion and confirmation; they teach Religious Education to children who are not attending Catholic schools; and lead the children's liturgy on Sunday during Mass

- **Welcomers, ushers and hospitality** who welcome people as they arrive for Mass; ushering them; providing hospitality on special occasions and for coffee mornings; acting as collectors and money counters

- **Parish administrators** who assist in the parish office, answer the phone in the presbytery, help maintain the parish database and registers, prepare and produce the newsletter, booklets, website, etc.

- **Cleaners, electricians, gardeners and builders** who maintain the church and the property around it and those who care for the church and grounds.

Parishes should encourage partnership by ensuring that volunteers:

- have a clear understanding of their role and know who they can go to for support (often called a volunteer contact person or ministry coordinator)

- are provided with a general introduction to what is happening in the parish and what services are on offer to people

- have access to training in their volunteer role, which shows volunteers that the parish takes their role seriously

- have the opportunity to develop their work in the parish and to take on new volunteer roles

- are trained as an equal partner with paid staff in the parish

- are offered a pathway for learning to ensure both initial and ongoing formation; for example, local classes in flower arranging, musicianship, administration and leadership skills are often available at reasonable cost, while deanery training and formation may be available through the diocese

- are listened to and consulted, receiving support and feedback

- know that they can volunteer for a particular term (months or years) if they wish.

The parish asks volunteers to:

- carry out agreed tasks

- take part in relevant training or on-going training or in annual days of recollection

- let the volunteer contact-person or ministry coordinator know if they are temporarily unavailable or if they change their address or phone number

- let the contact-person know if they no longer wish to volunteer.

It can be helpful if volunteers receive a written summary of what is expected of them when their service commences, as well as a summary of what the parish undertakes to provide for them. Contact phone numbers of the volunteer contact or coordinator, and of the parish priest might be included with this initial information pack. Those whose voluntary work involves the taking on of a public ministry in the parish are usually commissioned for that ministry at a liturgy (possibly Sunday Mass), at which parishioners are invited to support and pray for the ministers.

An example of the "job description" one diocese uses for volunteers who lead the Liturgy of the Word for Children during Sunday Mass follows. (This could be reproduced in a parish newsletter.)

Diocese of [insert location]

Job description: leaders of the Liturgy of the Word for Children

Role: leader of the Liturgy of the Word for Children on Sundays
Responsible to: [the parish priest/his delegate]
Aim: to lead pre-school and primary school children in a Liturgy of the Word adapted to their ability during Mass on Sundays

Main responsibilities:
- to work with other leaders of the group and to attend regular planning meetings
- to inform the parents and the parish community of the aim and content of the liturgy group
- to prepare the venue and clear it up after the celebration of the Word
- to ensure the safety and well-being of the children
- to liaise with the priest presiding and any other liturgical ministers at the Mass
- to provide the necessary books and equipment with the support of the parish
- to work together to ensure that the Liturgy is conducted in accordance with the Diocesan Safeguarding Procedures
- to monitor good practice and implement changes where necessary to enhance both the quality of the Liturgy and the safety of the children.

Person specification:
- the ability to relate with respect and ease to children and adults
- to enjoy working with children
- commitment to the essential teachings of the Catholic Church and the ethos of the parish
- a willingness to give time to the preparation of the sessions and the coordination of the group
- to be over 18 years of age if you are responsible for a group
- to undergo an Enhanced Disclosure Check from the DBS (Disclosure and Barring Service) or submit a Garda Vetting Form (ROI).

Meeting the needs of volunteers

Volunteers in the parish are likely to be covered by the parish's insurance policy for anything related to the voluntary work they are doing. This includes public liability and personal accident cover. If volunteers use their own car for parish work or if they use it to give anyone a lift, they will need to check that their car insurance covers this. There is not normally a problem, as long as the insurer is made aware of the fact – and no additional premium should be charged.

If a volunteer's work involves expenses, the parish will normally reimburse these. For example, if volunteers buy flowers, or use their cars, there will be a way to submit the receipt to the parish secretary or someone else to get these expenses paid. If volunteers think attendance at a course would be helpful, or need to buy books for catechetical programmes, they should ask the parish priest or coordinator for approval in advance – depending on what is involved.

Volunteers' agreement with the parish

Volunteers in the parish are expected to work within the parish's standard policies on volunteering, gender, HIV/AIDS, health and safety, child safeguarding and equal opportunities. These should be made available to volunteers by their volunteering contact or ministry coordinator. If volunteers have contact with children or vulnerable adults, they must submit to security checks, in accordance with diocesan safeguarding policy.

Volunteers' commitment of time in the parish can range from a few days each year to five days a week – depending on what volunteer work they are doing.

Volunteers should be realistic about how much they can do and shouldn't take on more than they can manage. In addition, volunteering should not seem like a life sentence! Parishes are very grateful for the time volunteers give the parish and it is important that volunteers should feel free to give up when they want to. Volunteers should tell their volunteering contact if they decide to stop volunteering so that the parish does not continue to rely on their work.

Conflict resolution

Volunteers, parish priests and volunteer contacts need to know how to tackle problems if things are going wrong – and they need to know who they can discuss issues with. One of the most challenging roles of an effective leader (whether they are the parish priest or a lay leader in the parish) is that of "peacekeeper". Resolving conflicts in the parish takes negotiation skills, patience, and a healthy dose of emotional intelligence.

A recognised model of conflict resolution model involves six basic steps and three golden rules. Susan Steinbrecher,[1] a mediator and speaker in leadership training, tells us that, in any dialogue, there are two fundamental needs that must be met – the ego need and the practical need. The ego needs are: to be listened to, valued, appreciated, empathised with, involved, and empowered. The practical need refers to the obvious: the reason for having the discussion that focuses on the conflict that needs to be solved.

To address both needs, there are the Three Golden Rules of Engagement:

1. Listen and respond with empathy.

2. Be involved; ask for the other person's opinions, ideas and thoughts.

3. Maintain and affirm self-esteem.

Keep in mind that if people don't feel that they are heard and appreciated, they will not be motivated or resolve to change. It's about compliance versus commitment. Without question, the person involved in the discussion or conflict resolution will be far more committed to the outcome if they have shared in the decision-making. As you go through the following six-step process, look for ways to weave in the golden rules: listening and responding with empathy, maintaining or affirming self-esteem and involving the person or people.

1. Be respectful in your discussions.

2. Be clear about the issue.

3. Discuss how the conflict (or problem) affects you, your group or the community.

4. Ask for the specific cause of the conflict (keeping in mind the ego needs).

5. Ask for the solution (keeping in mind the practical needs).

6. Agree on the action to be taken.

For example, at a newly formed liturgy group meeting which was preparing for the Easter Vigil, it became clear that the organist expected to plan the liturgy and to choose the music which she would play and her choir would sing. She argues that they've always done it. There was no need for specially printed booklets: the leaflets that had been used for years were just fine – and she'd put the hymn numbers up on the board, or the choir would sing for the congregation. But, there was a new liturgy group in the parish, whose role was to plan liturgical celebrations in partnership with the musicians and all other liturgical ministers because liturgy is bigger than the music alone. They wanted to make a booklet for the Easter Vigil so that the whole community could participate in the liturgy. Add to the mix another music group in the parish, which uses a keyboard, a guitar and drums. They play contemporary music drawn from the scripture of the day, as opposed to the more traditional music of the other group.

The discussion can easily get off on the wrong foot if each of the music groups feels superior to the other, or that their choice of music is better than the others. It can help enormously if you begin by being clear about the issue(s) and invite each of them to say how they think the problem can be solved. It is worth inviting the others present to discuss how the conflict (or struggle) has an impact on both of the groups; and how it affects the parish community (since the whole community comes together on this occasion and their preferences are divided). By asking both groups what they think the cause of the conflict is, you are meeting their ego needs to be listened to, valued, etc.

By asking them what the solution might be, you are meeting their practical need. Hopefully, they will come to the conclusion that there is room for both the more traditional and more modern at the same celebration. Getting the choir and the folk group to lead the singing together might also enhance the music – and, by practising together, a good partnership between them and respect for one another could develop. They may even conclude that they are "singing from the same hymn sheet" – and what they both have in common is their desire to enhance the liturgy and serve the community!

When this kind of heart-centred approach to conflict resolution is engaged, more often than not, it can make the difference between positive and negative outcomes. Leaders in church and in business benefit by learning this kind of communication, which comes from a place of respect for self and others. In promoting conflict resolution in the parish, it can sometimes be helpful to seek the advice and help of an independent mediator: your local diocesan office or pastoral planning department can usually supply useful contact numbers.

In his encyclical at the beginning of the new millennium Pope John Paul II wrote:

The Church of the Third Millennium will need to encourage all the baptised and confirmed to be aware of their active responsibility in the Church's life. Together with the ordained ministry, other ministries, whether formally instituted or simply recognised, can flourish for the good of the whole community, sustaining it in all its many needs: from catechesis to liturgy, from the education of the young to the widest array of charitable works.

Novo Millenio Ineunte, 46

POINTS TO REMEMBER

- We all have an important role to play in our parish and in our Church.

- Every person in the parish is uniquely gifted to volunteer in the parish and to enable Christ's Church to grow – and every person should feel welcome to offer their gifts.

- One of the most challenging roles of an effective leader is that of "peacekeeper". Resolving conflicts takes negotiation skills, patience, and a healthy dose of emotional intelligence.

POINTS FOR PERSONAL REFLECTION OR GROUP DISCUSSION

- Reflect on the role of volunteers in your parish and on the importance of their role.

- How are the needs of the volunteers in your parish met? Is there a volunteers' agreement? Does everyone feel they are welcome to offer their gifts?

- Think of a "peacekeeper" in your parish, family or work environment and reflect on how s/he resolves conflicts.

 Reflection

Teach us, good Lord,
to serve you as you deserve;
to give and not to count the cost;
to fight and not to heed the wounds;
to toil and not to seek for rest;
to labour and not to ask for any reward,
save that of knowing that we do your will.

A prayer of St Ignatius Loyola

ENDNOTES

[1] Susan Steinbrecher and Joel Bennett, *Heart-Centered Leadership: lead well, live well* (Sustainable Path Publishing, Hurst, Texas, 2014).

CHAPTER 4

PARISH EMPLOYEES: *Co-workers with priests*

Laity today are making an unprecedented response to the call of their baptism to serve God and the People of God in the Church in ways other than as a cleric. There are a growing number of paid pastoral apostolates in our parishes today, such as pastoral assistants, catechists, musicians and youth leaders. There are also many laypeople employed in our parishes as secretaries, bookkeepers, parish administrators, cleaners and maintenance workers. (This latter group are not necessarily Catholic – or practising Catholics – although they would normally be required to support the Catholic ethos of the parish and to be loyal to its aims and objectives.)

Pastoral workers are prepared by theological training, work experience and other formation appropriate to the level of responsibility of their ministry. They often bring with them many transferable gifts, talents and skills from their work in the secular world. We call them ministries because they participate in Jesus' mission to teach, sanctify and guide the community. This group of laity can be distinguished from the general body of the lay faithful, not by reason of merit or rank, but by reason of a call to service made possible by certain gifts of the Holy Spirit and by the generous response of the person.

How to get a paid job in a Catholic parish

If you wish to get paid employment in a parish, you need to acquire the necessary formation and skills for the role you want. For example, if you want to be a pastoral assistant, you may need to study theology at a level appropriate for the work you hope to do. If you want to be a catechist, find out what courses are available nationally or in your diocese; and, while you are following the courses, you might volunteer to help in a catechetical programme since there's no substitute for learning on the job. If you want to be a music minister, attend any music and liturgy workshops and do any courses that are available to you so that you will be informed about the various styles of church music and how to choose the most appropriate music for the different liturgical seasons. It is important to realise that working in a Catholic parish is very different from working in a commercial environment – indeed, we hope it is! Of course, there are things they all have in common in terms of the need for good timekeeping, communication, accountability, skill sets, etc. But, this job is built upon strong Christian foundations. Its purpose should be clear; it should be informed by beliefs and values that are rooted in scripture and Church teaching – and this should permeate every aspect of your

day-to-day work. However, just because the job is in a parish, it doesn't make the day-to-day logistics any easier to manage. Also, it doesn't necessarily make the people who work in it any holier than anyone else (or any easier to get along with).

Ready to apply for a job?

If you think you are ready to apply for a postition, find out what jobs are available by looking in *The Tablet* and other Catholic newspapers for advertisements. Look at diocesan websites too; more and more jobs are advertised there; occasionally you will see a position advertised in the local papers also. Once you've found a job you want to apply for, the first thing to do is to get to know the parish. Have a look at their website and read the parish's mission statement. Attend Mass in the parish and then decide if you feel "called" to work there. You might ask to look around the parish in advance of the interview, and you should certainly be offered a tour on the day itself. If at any point, you decide it is not for you, you can withdraw. It is important to be honest. If you are truthful and tactful, it should be respected and honoured.

During the enquiry period and interview, remember that it is as much about you getting a sense of the parish and the parish priest and deciding whether you will be comfortable in the job, as it is for the panel and parish priest getting a sense of you. It is a two-way process. The top tip for the application is to "be yourself". You don't have to pretend you are someone you are not. The selection panel will welcome honesty. From the outset, be clear about why you want this job and what you will bring to the role that will make a difference.

Many interview panels will ask you how you would support the mission statement of the parish, so it's worth making sure you look at it and have a few thoughts ready. You don't need to blind anyone with theological insights; but show some understanding of what the parish stands for. (This advice is especially important for non-Catholics, or indeed non-practising Catholics, who are applying for jobs in the parish.) And, remember that, if you are offered the job you are applying for, you will be representing the parish – so dress appropriately on the interview for the job you are applying for!

Advice for a parish thinking about hiring a layperson

If you are a parish priest and you want to hire a layperson to work in the parish, there are a number of things to think about. You might have someone in mind from the parish, but, before making up your mind, consider the following:

- Be transparent. Advertise the job to ensure that you employ the most qualified person.

- Consider employing someone who does not live in the parish. Managing someone who lives in your parish is not always easy. If there are any disciplinary problems, it is more awkward to deal with one of your parishioners than it is to deal with another employee.

- Contact your diocesan office or diocesan adviser; s/he may know of people who are looking for a job and may have valuable background information to offer.

- Your adviser can provide you with a sample job description and tell you what you can expect of your employee in terms of the hours they can and should work. They can advise on what salary and what benefits to offer.

- Your adviser can tell you what qualifications and experience you should be looking for; and they can tell you what formation and training opportunities are available to you.

- Many placements are made on the basis of the applicant's potential; be aware of the need to do some "on the job" training and supervision to begin with.

- If the job involves working in more than one parish – or a parish with more than one church – make sure to explain how this will work.

- It can be useful to seek the advice of clergy or personnel in other parishes who have recently hired paid staff.

Your diocesan office should also be able to help you:

- prepare an advertisement and advise you on salary and benefit-matters

- provide a contract of employment for your coordinator

- arrange for salary payments to be made (depending on local diocesan arrangements)

- help you with the interviewing process by reviewing applications, assisting with shortlisting, arranging the interviews and doing the administration associated with this.

An advert for a director of music (or a liturgical coordinator) in a parish made up of two churches might look like this:

Director of Music

required in a [rural/urban] parish made up of two churches commencing [insert date].

Applications are invited from candidates with experience of preparing liturgies.

We are looking for a musician's musician to develop vocalists and instrumentalists who will be responsible for coordinating the music for parish celebrations, including marriages and funerals in both churches that make up this parish.

The successful candidate will have a sound knowledge of the Church's liturgy and the Catholic faith; will have formal music training; and will have the ability to be a team member.

Hours: 25 hours per week; holidays 21 days per annum (pro-rata).

Salary: [insert sum] p.a. negotiable; closing date for applications is [insert date].

For a job description and application, please contact [insert contact details].

One for a parish secretary or parish administrator
might be presented thus:

Parish Secretary/Parish Administrator

is required in this busy [insert location] parish to commence [insert date].

In addition to being responsible for the typical secretarial and administrative duties
such as handling general correspondence, diary management and
general administration tasks, the ability to interact with parishioners visiting
the office and those involved in parish activities is essential.

The successful candidate will have experience; must have excellent communication
and office and computer skills (including Microsoft Word, Publisher and Excel).

Applicants are required to support the Catholic ethos of the parish,
to be loyal to the aims and objectives of the parish,
must be self-motivated, organised, be able to multi-task
and work to deadlines as well as the ability to be a team member
and to work on their own initiative in this role.
Hours: 37 ½ hours per week; holidays 21 days per annum.
Salary: [insert sum] p.a. negotiable; closing date [insert date].
For a job description and application,
please contact [insert contact details].

For parishes who don't want to go into so much detail, an advert might look like this:

Catechetical Coordinator needed in this [rural/urban] parish

to work with the parish priest and pastoral team with responsibility for developing, supporting and coordinating catechetical and sacramental programmes and courses to facilitate growth in the spiritual and catechetical life of the parish.

The successful candidate will be a practising and committed Catholic with relevant training and experience.

Hours of work: 20 hours per week (to include evenings and weekends).
Salary: [insert sum] an hour (negotiable); closing date [insert date].

For a job description and application,
please contact [insert contact details].

Notice that the advert for the pastoral jobs will normally stipulate that the successful candidate will be a practising and committed Catholic, whereas the advert for the parish secretary/parish administrator stipulates "support for" and "loyal to" the Catholic ethos of the parish. This is because it is not necessary for the person who fills some roles to be a Catholic (or a practising one) but they must be "in sympathy" with the Church to play a role in the parish.

An example of a job description for a parish catechetical coordinator might look like this:

Diocese of [insert location]

Job Description

Role: Catechetical Coordinator for [insert name of parish/parishes] parish or parishes
Responsible to: the Parish Priest
Aim: to assist in coordinating the work of parish catechesis

Pastoral duties and responsibilities:
*   to assist in the coordination of catechetics and related celebrations of liturgies
*   to assist in the coordination of lay ministers and parish volunteers
*   develop and maintain good parish communications
*   participate in Parish Pastoral Council.

Person specification:
*   to be a practising and committed Catholic in good standing with the Church
*   to work within the Diocesan Safeguarding Policies, and undergo an Enhanced Disclosure Check from the DBS (Disclosure and Barring Service) or submit Garda Vetting Form (ROI).

Catechetical duties and responsibilities:
*   to coordinate and promote catechetical programmes in the parish, including: baptism preparation for adults (RCIA) and parents of infants, First Communion and reconciliation, confirmation, religious education for children not in Catholic schools, adult formation
*   to coordinate and train volunteer catechists and helpers in the parish
*   to coordinate and develop children's participation in liturgy
*   to encourage catechists to reflect on the General Directory for Catechesis (GDC)
*   to liaise with the parish priest and the community on catechetical matters
*   to support and promote initiatives for the development of youth work in the parish.

Parish administration:
- to assist with any correspondence, booklet preparation and filing as needed
- other general office duties, i.e. photocopying, ordering stationery, etc.
- to answer the door and greet visitors
- diary management for catechetical programmes, parish appointments, events
- any ad hoc duties as required, including assisting with pastoral matters
- to organise and provide all materials needed by catechists and volunteers.

Competencies required:
- ability to work in a small team mostly comprising volunteers under the supervision of the parish priest
- organisational skills and the ability to prioritise and meet deadlines
- ability to listen and to motivate and instil enthusiasm into others
- to adhere to the diocesan safeguarding policy
- to have some knowledge and practice of pastoral ministry
- to have a sound understanding of the doctrinal, social and moral teaching of the Catholic Church and adherence to its faith and morals
- to be able to maintain confidentiality.

In some dioceses, you will be employed by the parish itself (especially if the parish is run by a religious community); in others you will be employed by the diocese for responsibility to work in a particular parish or parishes. Either way, you should be given an employment contract. These contracts do not have to be in writing to be legally valid, but it is better if they are.

Key points to be aware of:

- A contract of employment is an agreement between an employer and employee and is the basis of the employment relationship. It can only be varied with the agreement of both parties.

- A contract "starts" as soon as an offer of employment is accepted. Starting work proves that you accept the terms and conditions offered by the employer.

- Most employees are legally entitled to a Written Statement of the main terms and conditions of employment within two calendar months of starting work. This should include:

- name of employer and employee

- date employment and continuous employment started and the job location

- job description/job title

- details of any agreements that directly affect the employee's conditions of employment

- pay and whether it's weekly or monthly pay etc.

- working hours/holiday entitlement

- additional information can be provided in this statement or in other documents such as staff handbooks, sick leave and pay entitlements, pensions and pension schemes, disciplinary and grievance procedures appeals.

All this may appear legalistic; but it is important for the parish priest and employee to be aware of legal rights and obligations. Remember: many priests and people who apply to work in parishes have no experience of employment – and it is not always easy for a lay employee to ask these questions or for a parish priest to know all the answers (especially one who is new in this role).

A sense of being on equal terms and of equal regard is vital in developing a culture of collaboration, but this is hard to achieve. The theory of working together on equal terms is difficult when one partner is ordained and the other is not, when one has more (or different) training, resources and recognition than the other; and there are tensions as both together (with mutual respect for one another) make use of different skills and knowledge.

It is hard to feel that there is equal valuing; and tensions arise from the different financial situations; for example, the possible tensions between a priest who is full-time and has living expenses supplied and a layperson who is full-time but whose paid salary will not support the same standard of living as the priest.

Although the theology of communion implies equal valuing based on personhood and gift, we live in a world that measures value in other ways and we cannot be unaffected by it.

We will see many changes in the next couple of decades. As vocations to the ordained priesthood fall, more and more laypeople are taking full-time ministerial and leadership roles in the Church. The fact is that we are still in the early stages of learning how to work together in the Church; and it is not always easy to work with others.

Myers Briggs: one possible key to working well with others

Each of us is unique; and, although some of our characteristics are shared with other people, others are not. Knowing ourselves is the work of a lifetime, but knowing about those similarities and differences can help deepen self-awareness and improve relationships. Kit Dollard has a special interest in this area. He sometimes facilitates difficult situations by using, as a starting point or guide, the Myers Briggs Type Indicator (MBTI®).[1] Based on the theory of psychological types developed by Carl Jung, it helps to explain some of the differences in people's behaviour which can help you see why you argue with the same people about the same things, why some things drain us and others give us energy, why it is so difficult to make decisions – or why you like to pray in a particular way and you're put off by other ways.

The MBTI has helped people understand their personality and their spirituality for more than fifty years. Jung observed two opposite ways of perceiving, which he called sensing and intuition, and two opposite ways of judging, which he called thinking and feeling. In addition, a pattern will emerge that reflects a personal preference for sources of energy and these Jung identified as extrovert and introvert. The MBTI addresses four questions in order to determine people's personality type.

The first question asks if you are an **extrovert** – someone who is energised through activities outside yourself; **introverts**, on the other hand, are energised by the inner world; typically they are likely to remain silent in a talkative meeting.

The second question asks how you process information. If you focus on what you know, on clarity and facts involving the five senses, your personality type is likely to be that of a **sensor**; whereas, if you are **intuitive**, you prefer to focus on ideas and inspirations, and trust your sixth sense: you are someone who doesn't worry about the details but looks at the bigger picture.

The third question relates to how you prefer to make decisions. The **thinker** prefers logical, objective reasoning, as opposed to the **feeler** whose world is dominated by harmony, empathy and values. A feeler will perceive conflict or argument while two thinkers enjoy a heated discussion.

Finally, the fourth question relates to how you prefer to organise your life. **Judgers** prefer to make decisions, to control, to set goals and strive for closure. **Perceivers** prefer to adapt, to go with the flow, to seek options and are flexible. Judgers need schedules and plans while for perceivers, tomorrow is soon enough.

For an example of how an MBTI workshop might work, imagine a parish where the staff consists of a parish priest, an assistant priest, a catechetical coordinator and a parish secretary. The catechetical coordinator is passionate about her work and an intuitive thinker. The majority of the other staff members are sensing feelers. As a result of her inability to communicate her passion effectively to the parish priest and the others, the catechist was always losing out. In particular, a proposed idea for an exhibition and workshop on prayer through iconography was dismissed as something nobody in the parish was likely to come to.

As a result of the MBTI session, the parish team recognises the insights of the catechist. The spiritual emphasis in the parish shifts to being more intuitive – more imaginative, open to change, focusing on the symbolic and a greater creativity in prayer, liturgies and catechetical sessions.

 POINTS TO REMEMBER

- ☑ No one knows everything they need to know when they begin working in a parish – so don't be afraid to ask if you don't know something.
- ☑ Whether you are looking for a job or you are looking for an employee, begin the process with prayer and ask the right people for advice.
- ☑ We are all human and it is not always easy to work with others. Understanding your own personality and the personality of others can help.

POINTS FOR PERSONAL REFLECTION
OR GROUP DISCUSSION

- ⚔ What did you know about parish work before you started working in the parish and what was your source of knowledge?
- ⚔ What is your experience – positive or negative – about working in the Church? If you have questions or concerns about it, where can you go for answers? Who can you go to?
- ⚔ We are all on a journey; right now, you are here because you have been chosen.

Reflection

God has created me to do him some definite service. He has committed some work to me which He has not committed to another. I have my mission. I may never know it in this life, but I shall be told it in the next. I am a link in a chain, a bond of connection between persons.
He has not created me for naught. I shall do good; I shall do his work.

I shall be an angel of peace, a preacher of truth in my own place, while not intending it, if I do but keep his commandments.

Therefore, I will trust him; whatever I am I can never be thrown away.

*Blessed John Henry Newman,
priest and theologian, (1801–1890)*

Prayer

Lord, take me where you want me to go;
let me meet who you want me to meet.
Tell me what you want me to say –
and keep me out of your way.

*Prayer of Fr Mychal Judge, chaplain to the
New York City Fire Department who died on
11 September 2001 after being hit by falling
debris from the World Trade Center as he gave the
Last Rites to an injured firefighter*

ENDNOTES

[1] MBTI® may not suit everyone. Article based on a Parish Practice article by Kit Dollard, "It's not all left to chance", *The Tablet*, 28 June 2014.

CHAPTER 5

LITURGIES: *They don't just fall into place*

Christian liturgy in the early Church

A detailed description of Christian Eucharist is found in the work of St Justin, martyred in the middle of the second century. In his defence of Christian practices (*Apologia*) to the Emperor, he described the weekly celebration, which he says takes place "on the day called Sunday":

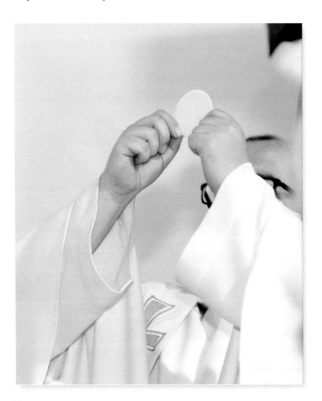

On the day called Sunday,
all who live in cities or in the country
gather together to one place,
and the memoirs of the apostles
or the writings of the prophets are read,
as long as time permits.
Then, when the reader has ceased,
the president verbally instructs us, and
exhorts to the imitation of these good things.
Then we all stand up together and pray.
When our prayer is ended, bread and wine
and water are brought forward.
The president offers prayers
and gives thanks to the best of his ability,
and the people give assent by saying, "Amen".
The Eucharist is distributed,
everyone present communicates,
and the deacons take it to those who are absent.
The wealthy, if they wish, may make a contribution,
and they themselves decide the amount.
The collection is placed in the custody of the president,
who uses it to help the orphans and widows
and all who for any reason are in distress, whether
because they are sick, in prison,
or away from home.
In a word, he takes care of all who are in need.

St Justin, *Apologia*, Chapter 67 [1]

From Justin's writings certain elements in the Eucharist are clear: there is a Liturgy of the Word and a Liturgy of the Eucharist, an offertory, a Eucharistic Prayer (although it would seem there were no set prayers), Communion, and a collection (one tradition that has remained steadfastly unchanged through the centuries!). If you are interested in reading more about how the early Church celebrated the Eucharist, you can find it in Acts of the Apostles and in St Justin's *Apologia*.[2]

Catholic liturgy since Vatican II

A significant way that the Second Vatican Council transformed the Church was in the way we experience and better understand the mystery of God as our own mystery. *Sacrosanctum Concilium* reformed our liturgies – calling for a "fully conscious, and active participation [of all people] in liturgical celebrations" (SC 14). We came to understand that liturgy is an important point of encounter between God and his people.

Since these reforms took place, we have also recovered a better awareness of the liturgical nature of the Church's pastoral ministry. Catholics support one another as they celebrate Christian marriage – just as they support priests and deacons when they are ordained. We have a new order for Christian initiation which eventually brings new believers to the fullness of the Liturgy of the Eucharist. When Christians die, the reformed rites provide for the assembling of believers to pray to commend the deceased publicly to God's mercy. And, we pray for the absent sick and elderly in our general intercessions; we send ministers to the sick and the elderly who cannot come to Mass as a sign that they are one with us at the Eucharistic table.

We have also discovered the power of faith-sharing in small Christian communities. People meet together to pray, to read a passage of the Gospel and to reflect on the circumstances of their daily lives. One single truth – a single mystery – where we can encounter Christ is being set out in a variety of liturgical celebrations when the Church is assembled in the mystery of Christ. God wants to be present to us. He wants to have a relationship with us; he wants us to encounter him. This chapter will tell you the "who, what, where, how, why and when" you need to know when planning *key* liturgies; it will address some of the issues; it will tell you about good practice in parishes.

Planning a liturgy

The very first time a newly ordained priest friend of mine asked me to organise a Mass for him, I invited all his friends to come along and I made sure the chapel was free that evening. It didn't occur to me that he was expecting me to prepare the chapel, find readers, choose hymns, etc. We've included this section in order to help priests and laypeople to speak the same language! Whether the liturgy will be a Eucharistic one or a non-eucharistic one, here are some important notes about planning a liturgy that you should bear in mind:

Before the day

Make sure you have arranged for the priest or liturgical leader to be present and that you have discussed the celebration with him/her. With liturgical (and prayer) celebrations, it is always helpful to have everything in writing for everyone involved. For example:

- Who will be taking part? Who will be leading the liturgy? Who else will be involved? Does everyone know who and what is involved?

- When and where will the liturgy take place? Make sure everyone knows.

- If the liturgy is a Mass or a Liturgy of the Word with Holy Communion, check the Liturgical Calendar (the *Ordo*) for your diocese to see if the day is a Memorial, Feast, or Solemnity. Be aware that the readings for certain days should never be changed; you should ask if you are unsure.

- Unless the liturgy has a theme which does not marry with the readings of the day, it is preferable to use the readings of the day. If you want to change the readings, make sure the priest or leader is in agreement.

- Will you have music? If so, check to see who is leading and choosing the music. Coordination is necessary; the music chosen should complement the scripture readings.

On the day

Readers should prepare before the liturgy begins. If the liturgical celebration is a Eucharistic one, you should use the translation used in the Catholic Lectionary from the *Jerusalem Bible*. Although it is acceptable to simplify a scripture passage for young children or people with learning disabilities, adaptations of scripture should not be used in liturgical celebrations.

Silence is an integral element of liturgy. The whole way in which liturgy is celebrated should foster reflectiveness; it requires short intervals of silence. Servers and sacristans should be prepared well since they are the ones who will ensure that all requisites for the celebration are available at the appropriate moments.

If your liturgy is taking place outside of the church and it is being led by a priest, make sure you ask him to bring his vestments. Remember that they are colour-coded according to the season or feast. The basics are an *alb* (a plain white tunic), a *stole* (which the priest wears around his neck) and a *chasuble* (an outer garment).

It is important that the place where the Church gathers for worship is clean and tidy and fit for its purpose. The place should be decorated in an appropriate way to complement the liturgy.

If you are celebrating a Eucharistic liturgy outside of the church, you will need:

- an altar (a table covered with a white cloth), a chalice, paten (or plate), altar crucifix and two candles, wine and breads

- two smaller white cloths: a corporal for the paten and chalice to rest on and a purificator to wipe the lip of the chalice between one person and the next receiving Communion

- a bowl of water and a towel

- a chair for the priest, a credence table for the sacred vessels and cruets for water and wine

- flowers are optional (and remember that no flowers are used in Lent)

- a lectern, a stand which holds the lectionary (the book containing the scripture readings)

- the Roman Missal.

If this Eucharistic liturgy outside of the church is celebrated in a home, usually the house is blessed at the start of Mass; in this case, a bowl of (unblessed) water is provided, together with a small branch of palm or a similar tree for the sprinkling.

If you are celebrating a non-eucharistic liturgy inside or outside of the church, you should create a special place with a focal point in which might be placed:

- the Bible (or a lectionary from which the reading will be proclaimed)

- an icon, crucifix and candles, concrete reminders that Jesus is with us.

Planning a Eucharistic liturgy: the structure of the Mass:

- **the Gathering Rite** which includes a welcome by the priest, the Penitential Rite, the Gloria (on Sundays, feast days and on holy days of obligation, but not on ordinary weekdays or on Sundays in Advent or Lent) and the Collect of the Mass

- **the Liturgy of the Word** which includes the first reading, a psalm in response to it, a second reading (on Sundays and holy days), the Gospel Acclamation (normally the Alleluia except for Lent) and the Gospel followed by the homily, the profession of faith or the Creed and the general intercessions

- **the Liturgy of the Eucharist** which includes the presentation of the gifts, the Eucharistic Prayer, the Lord's Prayer (the Our Father), the sign of peace, the Lamb of God (the *Agnus Dei*) and Holy Communion

- **the Concluding Rites** which include the concluding prayers and blessing.

Planning a non-eucharistic liturgy or a prayer service:

The structure of a non-eucharistic liturgy will vary, but it is likely to include:

- **a Gathering Rite** and a welcome by the liturgical leader

- **a Liturgy of the Word** – a reading or readings and a reflection on the readings followed by prayers of intercession

- **a Concluding Rite** which includes the concluding prayers/blessing.

Planning a Liturgy of the Word with Holy Communion

It is becoming more common all over the world for the community to gather and celebrate the word of God and distribute Holy Communion in the absence of a priest. In fact, the National Conference of Catholic Bishops in the US approved a rite for this eventuality in 1994, entitled "Sunday Celebrations in the Absence of a Priest". At present, these celebrations are rare on Sundays here (although they are becoming more and more common elsewhere). The frequency, availability and format of these celebrations may be a matter of diocesan policy which should be observed.[3]

The preparation of the whole parish for these celebrations is of vital importance – and for the ministers involved to be offered liturgical and spiritual formation. In particular, those who will lead these liturgies should be chosen with care, be recognised by and acceptable to the parish. A lay leader will be assisted by other ministers such as a reader, minister of Communion, musician (since it is recommended that the leader should not do everything). The leader reads the Gospel, reflects on it and ministers Holy Communion. Other lay members of the community read the scripture readings before the Gospel. They may also announce the intentions for prayer in the general intercessions, and, as necessary, they assist in distributing Holy Communion.

Where the leader is not a commissioned minister of Communion, a minister of Communion leads the prayer from the Lord's Prayer until after the distribution. The vesture and gestures of the leader are not distinctive lest this celebration be confused with the Mass. It should also be noted that the leader does not preside from the ambo and altar.

Where the community has the service of a deacon, who has been ordained for the nurture and increase of the People of God, he will preside and preach at these liturgies.

Before you lead the celebration you should do the following:

- check the Ordo (liturgical calendar) for your diocese to see if the day is a Memorial, Feast, or Solemnity and set the Lectionary for the readings of the day

- check the Roman Missal to see if a Collect is assigned to the particular day and

- prepare anything you will say in the celebration that is not scripted, for instance, introductory remarks, reflection on the readings, intercessions, concluding announcements.

The structure of the liturgy:

- **the Introductory Rites** which include the greeting and introduction, the Penitential Act, the Gloria and the Collect

- **the Liturgy of the Word** which includes the reading, the psalm, the Gospel Acclamation, the Gospel (a lay leader omits the greeting before the Gospel), the reflection followed by silence, the Profession of Faith, the Prayer of the Faithful and the Act of Thanksgiving (a psalm or hymn of praise, sung or spoken)

- **the Liturgy of Communion** which includes the transfer of the Blessed Sacrament, the Lord's Prayer, the Sign of Peace, and Communion, followed by silence and the Prayer after Communion

- **the Concluding Rites** which includes the announcements, collection, blessing and dismissal.

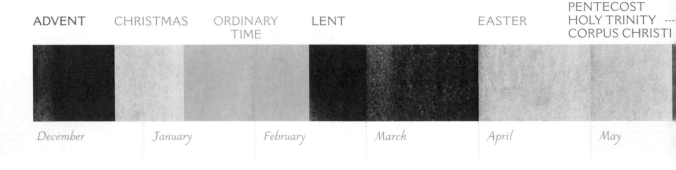

ADVENT	CHRISTMAS	ORDINARY TIME	LENT	EASTER	ASCENSION PENTECOST HOLY TRINITY CORPUS CHRISTI
December	January	February	March	April	May

 Advent

Liturgical colour: purple

Dates: late November/early December, ending on 24 December

Advent is the season of preparation to meet Christ, both in the celebration of his birth and his Second Coming. It is a penitential season and many parishes organise penitential services during this time. The themes of the season are: "Wake up!", "Prepare the way of the Lord", "Rejoice" and "Emmanuel is with us". These are sometimes translated as hope, joy, love and peace.

For Catholics, the call to work for charity and the common good is heightened at times like Advent and Lent. It is a time for personal renewal, growth and transformation. God has heard the cry of the poor and comes and Jesus came to save, heal and reconcile – that is a key message of Advent.

 Christmas

Liturgical colour: white

Dates: 25 December to the Baptism of the Lord (usually the Sunday after Epiphany)

At Christmas, Christians celebrate Emmanuel, from the Hebrew for "God with us". That, of course, took place in the form of the birth of Jesus. The Christmas season comes to a close after the feast of the Baptism of the Lord, which is usually held on the Sunday after Epiphany. (Epiphany falls on 6 January and is when Christians celebrate the coming of the magi, or wise men, to worship Jesus.) In some countries, including England, Wales and Scotland, the Epiphany is now celebrated on the second Sunday after Christmas.

July   August   September   October   November

Lent

Liturgical colour: purple

Dates: six weeks between Ash Wednesday and Easter Sunday

Lent reminds Christians of the forty days Jesus spent fasting and praying in the desert before he began his ministry (Matthew 4:1-11). It is when the Church prepares for the greatest of all celebrations: Easter. Because its focus is the lead-up to the death of Jesus, Lent is a serious time when the Church encourages us to pray, fast and abstain, and to give alms or do something for the good of the community.

Holy Week is the sixth week in Lent, and forms a dramatic climax to the period. It is when Christians really focus on the events leading up to the crucifixion of Jesus on Good Friday and the resurrection of Jesus on Easter Sunday. Many parishes organise penitential services and re-enactments in the form of passion plays or Stations of the Cross, which represent Jesus' journey to his crucifixion at Calvary.

There are subtle but important variations in the liturgy during Lent. For example, "Alleluia" is not used in worship during Lent – so be careful if you are the one choosing hymns and acclamations, and if in doubt, ask!

Easter

Liturgical colour: white or gold

Dates: a Sunday between 22 March and 25 April, and the following fifty days

This is a time of rejoicing and celebrating Christ's resurrection from the dead. It is about the triumph of good over evil, life over death. The mood is very different – and "Alleluia" is again sung and said.

Pentecost

Liturgical colour: red

Date: fiftieth day after Easter Day

Today, Christians focus on the descent of the Holy Spirit on the apostles (Acts 2:1-12). Red symbolises fire and the Holy Spirit. You may hear Pentecost referred to as Whit Sunday, or the birthday of the Church.

Holy days of obligation and other celebrations

The list on pages 54-55 outlines the main seasons, feast days, festivals and solemnities that you will come across in the life of the parish. There are also holy days of obligation on which the faithful are obliged to participate in the Mass and abstain from anything that prevents them from worshipping God. Every Sunday is a holy day of obligation and some of the other days are often celebrated on the nearest Sunday. Most parishes provide for a very early morning Mass or an evening Mass so that people who are working in offices or shops can get to Mass before or after their working hours. Anticipatory vigil masses may also be provided.

Holy days of obligation in England, Wales and Scotland

- Every Sunday

- 6 January: The Epiphany of the Lord (England and Wales) (transferred to the second Sunday after Christmas)

- The Ascension of the Lord (Thursday after the Sixth Sunday of Easter) (Scotland only)

- In the case of the following three holy days, if they fall on a Saturday or a Monday, the feast is celebrated on the Sunday:

- Ss Peter and Paul, Apostles: 29 June

- The Assumption of the Blessed Virgin Mary: 15 August

- All Saints: 1 November

- 25 December: Christmas Day

Holy days of obligation in Ireland

- Every Sunday

- 6 January: The Epiphany

- 17 March: St Patrick's Day

- 15 August: The Assumption of the Blessed Virgin Mary

- 1 November: All Saints' Day

- 8 December: The Immaculate Conception of the Blessed Virgin Mary

- 25 December: Christmas Day

Liturgical colours

These will be used in the sanctuary decoration and the priest's vestments to reflect the mood of the season. White, red, green, purple and gold are the most common you will see; but black and pink are also used. If you see red, for example, at a time other than Pentecost, it generally means that a martyr or apostle is being commemorated on that day. Similarly, the third Sunday of Advent is known as "Gaudete" (rejoice) Sunday, when the penitential purple gives way to rose or pink. This explains why you will see three purple candles and one pink candle on the Advent wreath.

Liturgical cycles

The start of a new liturgical year, beginning with the first Sunday of Advent, also marks the transition from one lectionary cycle (A, B, or C) to the next. These cycles are a result of the Second Vatican Council, which ordered a change in the Sunday readings at Mass so that Catholics would become more familiar with the text of the Bible.

As a result we now have a three-year cycle of readings built around readings from the three synoptic Gospels – Matthew, Mark, and Luke. In this section you can find information and activities related to each cycle:

Cycle A: the Gospel of Matthew

In the Year A (2017, 2020, etc.) in the Catholic Church's lectionary of scripture readings for Mass, the Gospel passage almost every Sunday is taken from St Matthew. We meet St Matthew only indirectly through the Gospel that bears his name.

Cycle B: the Gospel of Mark

In the Year B (2018, 2021, etc.), the Gospel of St Mark is featured prominently. Mark's Gospel is now generally regarded as the earliest Gospel. It presents a stark and challenging portrait of Jesus' public ministry, which leads into a dramatic account of his passion and death. It has often been described as a passion narrative with a long introduction. Mark presents Jesus as a wise teacher and a powerful and compassionate healer.

Cycle C: the Gospel of Luke

In the Year C (2019, 2022, etc.), the Gospel passage almost every Sunday is taken from St Luke. Like Matthew, we meet the person we call St Luke only indirectly. We do so primarily through the two books that have traditionally been ascribed to him: the Gospel according to Luke and the Acts of the Apostles.

POINTS TO REMEMBER

- ☑ A significant way that the Second Vatican Council transformed the Church was its call (SC 14) for "full, conscious, and active participation" (of all people) in liturgical celebrations.

- ☑ Everyone (priests and laypeople) are on a learning curve in their understanding of the liturgy and the sacraments and how best to celebrate them. If in doubt, ask for help.

- ☑ The liturgical seasons are times for focusing and refocusing us on what matters – the liturgy and the sacraments and how best to celebrate them. If in doubt, ask for help.

POINTS FOR PERSONAL REFLECTION OR GROUP DISCUSSION

- ⚊ Reflect on the similarities you can recognise between St Justin's account of a Eucharistic celebration in AD 150 and in your parish today.

- ⚊ Think of a liturgy that you've experienced that has some significance for you. What was it? And, why was it significant?

- ⚊ Do you experience a "full, conscious, and active participation" (of all people) in liturgical celebrations? Could you improve on this?

- ⚊ How would you evaluate the way your parish celebrates the liturgical year?

Prayer

God our Father,
your Son called disciples to follow him
and helped them understand his way:
Lead us to a deeper understanding
of the liturgy and the sacraments
and how best to celebrate them,
so that your people may grow in faith
and our communities be places
of ever-deepening love and peace.
Through Jesus Christ our Lord.
Amen.

ENDNOTES

[1] This famous passage from the *First Apology of St Justin Martyr* is used in the Office of Readings for the Third Sunday of Easter.

[2] If you are interested in reading more about the early Church, read:
- a translation of the *Apostolic Tradition* online (www.bombaxo.com/hippolytus.html)
- the first two chapters of Acts
- the *Didache* (www.earlychristianwritings.com/text/didache-roberts.html).

[3] For a full text, see the Bishops' Conference of England and Wales Liturgy Office website: www.liturgyoffice.org.uk/Resources/CWC/CWAC.pdf

CHAPTER 6
CATECHESIS 1: *What it means*

Helping us stay "connected" has become an imperative in our culture. Smartphones, Facebook, and Twitter give us instant access to friends, family, work, and the world. Many say that we spend less time building and maintaining meaningful face-to-face relationships as a result. The simple fact is that you cannot know someone you don't spend time with. Intimacy develops as a result of close contact with someone over a period of time. Trust is built, confidence grows, and hearts change, becoming endeared to one another.

We connect with others by spending time with them, talking to them and listening to them. We observe them, noticing how they react in different circumstances – what choices they make and how they "tick". And, we celebrate life with them – birthdays, anniversaries, holidays and so forth – those occasions that give meaning to our lives.

The very same dynamic is applied to what we do in catechesis. The purpose of catechesis is to be connected with Christ. We do this by spending time with Jesus in prayer and we speak with him; we listen to him in scripture – observing how he lived his life, how he responded to people, to their problems, to their needs, what moral values he taught them, what choices he made in his life.

Following the publication of *Dei Verbum* (Dogmatic Constitution on Divine Revelation), a new model of catechesis grew out of revelation as God's self-communication, which emphasises the need for our catechesis to be based on Christ and on scripture, doctrine and liturgy. These are the ways we can stay connected with God. The *Catechism of the Catholic Church* (CCC) makes the link between that and the four pillars of the Catechism: the profession of faith, the celebration of the liturgy, morality in the Gospel and, prayer. The *General Directory of Catechesis* (GDC) tells us that this is where the content of the faith is found (GDC 93). This is the basis of all our catechetical programmes in the parish. Anyone who wants to survive working in a Catholic parish has to know about catechesis and the process of our catechetical programmes.

The catechetical method
The Church, in transmitting the faith, does not have a particular method nor any single method. Rather, she uses "everything that is true, everything that is noble, everything that is good and pure, everything that we love and honour and everything that can be thought virtuous or worthy of praise" (Philippians 4:8). In short, she assumes those methods which are not contrary to the Gospel and places them at its service (GDC 148).

The praxis method is one of the more popular choices used in many catechetical programmes. It was developed by Tom Groome. He uses the story of the walk to Emmaus (Luke 24:13-23) as the basis of his praxis approach in religious education. Groome has drawn upon Freire's work in *Christian Religious Education*.[1] (Paulo Freire was, perhaps, the most influential thinker about dialogue, praxis and education in the late twentieth century.)

Groome reflects on Luke's Gospel:
On that first Easter Sunday, two of Jesus' followers were making their way to Emmaus, a small village about seven miles from Jerusalem. As they went their way, they discussed "all that had happened" (v14) over the previous days, and, as might be expected, it was a "lively exchange" (v15). Who should join them but the risen Jesus, who began "to walk along with them" (v15). For whatever reason, they were "restrained from recognising him" (v16). He entered into their company by inquiring, "What are you discussing along your way?" (v17). Somewhat distressed and a little impatient at the stranger's ignorance, they wondered where he had been. Surely, everyone in Jerusalem knew "the things that went on there during these past few days?" (v18). Rather than seizing this obvious opportunity to disclose his identity (who knew better than he what had gone on there?), he inquired, "What things?" (v19). They told him the story as they knew it and their dwindling hope that "he was the one who would set Israel free" (v21). Now, adding confusion to their disappointment, "some women" (v22) of the group were spreading the "astonishing news" (v22).

In this first movement of the method, we are invited to a personal or faith experience related to the theme of the catechetical session.

Jesus cajoled them for not looking at these recent events within a broader context, and in response to their story and hope, he told them an older *story* and a larger *vision*. "Beginning then, with Moses and all the prophets, he interpreted for them every passage of Scripture, which referred to him" (v27). He pointed out that the Messiah had to "undergo all this so as to enter into his glory" (v26). Surely now they would recognise him. They did not, and he continued to resist telling them. But he had obviously aroused their curiosity, for they "pressed him" (v29) to stay the night in their company. He agreed.

In this second movement of the method, we are invited to turn to scripture passages and to the Tradition of the Church – God's story sheds light on our own story. In our catechetical sessions, we will include: Doctrine, Scripture, Tradition, Liturgy and faith stories of our Catholic Church.

At table that evening, he blessed and broke bread for them and "with that their eyes were opened and they recognised him; whereupon he vanished from their sight" (v31). Then the pieces of their puzzle fell in place, and they remembered how their hearts had "burned" inside them as he talked "on the road". But instead of spending time in self-reproach for not seeing sooner, they set out immediately for Jerusalem (a hazardous journey by night) to tell "the Eleven and the rest of the company" (v33). They told the story of what had happened "on the road" and "how they had come to know him in the breaking of the bread" (v35).

In this third movement of the method, we are invited to dialogue between our story and God's story and to make a personal faith response. Like the disciples, we want to go out to bring the Good News to those we meet. [2]

Note: *Doctrine* is what the Church believes and teaches. It is the underpinning of faith. It is sometimes talked about as a "body of teaching" because, like a body, it has many different parts linked together in a single purpose of enabling life, in this case, the life of faith. The doctrine included in the sessions should be sufficient, but appropriate to the people involved. The teaching of the Church unfolds in history and it will unfold gradually in our lives (CCC 26).

Tradition refers to the living faith and doctrine received from the foundational experience and handed down through the ages in the Church (DV 8). When tradition is written with a small "t", it refers to traditions in the sense of family or cultural traditions, i.e. ways of doing things that are uniquely Catholic.

The Rite of Christian Initiation of Adults: the model for all catechesis

The *Rite of Christian Initiation of Adults* (RCIA) is credited with restoring the intimate relationship between catechesis and liturgy. Aware of the power of the catechumenate to both form and transform the People of God, the *General Directory for Catechesis* (GDC) makes the catechumenate the model for all catechesis in the Church. It is the process that we use in the RCIA when an adult is converted to faith through making an explicit profession of baptismal faith. It says that this model of faith formation should inspire other forms of catechesis in both their objectives and in their dynamism (GDC 59). The directive is clear. We have been given a whole new way of *doing catechesis* in the Church.

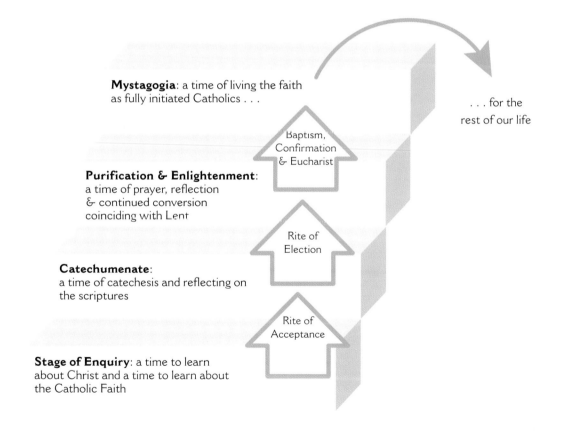

Mystagogia: a time of living the faith as fully initiated Catholics . . .

. . . for the rest of our life

Baptism, Confirmation & Eucharist

Purification & Enlightenment: a time of prayer, reflection & continued conversion coinciding with Lent

Rite of Election

Catechumenate: a time of catechesis and reflecting on the scriptures

Rite of Acceptance

Stage of Enquiry: a time to learn about Christ and a time to learn about the Catholic Faith

Jim Dunning, in his classic book, *Echoing God's Word*, challenged us to view the concept of *journeying* in catechesis; and told us that we (priests and catechists) need to take the journey ourselves. We need to taste the new wine and shed the old wineskins. He asserted that we, as ministers, must allow ourselves to be transformed if we are to help others be transformed. We need formation and transformation – not just information. We need both the *what* (the vision of the Church, faith, conversion, and liturgical catechesis in these rites) and also some *how* (some practical ways for pastoral ministers and catechumens to do that liturgical catechesis). [3]

In other words, we need to experience the methods that bring the word of God to echo in and through our lives. Christian initiation (and all Christian growth, for that matter) is a life-long *process* not a *programme*. Dunning draws upon the teaching of the well-known Jesuit philosopher Bernard Lonergan who compares the process which grounds the four periods in the RCIA as being parallel to some extent to the process of coming to insight: be *attentive* (tune your antennae into all the riches of your experience). Be *reflective* (plumb the meaning of all the data). Be *responsible* (be able to respond to what you discover). Be *loving* (share the gift with others). Enquiry, Dunning says, demands attention. Catechumenate demands reflection. Enlightenment demands response-ability. Mystagogia emerges from and into love. [4]

Is this not the journey of the disciples in Luke that we saw at the beginning of this chapter? They were walking to Emmaus *telling their story* and *reflecting* on that story. They listened to Jesus and they *shared the*

meaning of their tradition (Moses and all the prophets, who suffered and died because of their fidelity). There was conversion – their eyes were opened at the breaking of the bread; they turned around and rushed back to *share their Good News* with the other disciples.

These are the four periods of RCIA. They overlap just as Lonergan's imperatives overlap. The point here is that they are ingredients in a process of how people grow; and, because of their unique personal history, people will move at their own rate through the process. When the RCIA was first introduced, many elements of it were new to people. For example, the idea of making a choice *after* an appropriate time of formation – and spending time reflecting on what it was like to celebrate a sacrament. Not many Catholics have been assisted, after the celebration of *any* sacrament, in the work of more fully appropriating and owning the experience of the sacrament.

One of the major contributions of the RCIA is that it has broadened the whole concept of *celebration*. There are many festive moments other than the final celebration of water baptism, confirmation and admission to the table of the Eucharist. The time of enquiry, during which the candidate takes their first steps toward the Christian community, culminates in a ritual of enrolment, when one is formally joined to the Church. The time of formation, which might consist of months or years, culminates in the Rite of Election. This is a celebration of twofold choice that has come to term: the candidate's acceptance of the Christian community and the community's own acceptance of the candidate. The final period of preparation itself is marked by numerous rites of blessing and healing (the scrutinies, etc.) which are celebrated in the weeks preceding baptism. And then, they celebrate all three sacraments of initiation: baptism, confirmation and the Eucharist (normally at the Easter Vigil).

We turn now to the rest of this chapter to see how we can apply this catechetical process in our parish programmes.

Infant baptism

The birth of any child is an event in the life history of that child, of the parents and the extended family. When we welcome new life into the world, people often take the time to reflect on the meaning of life. Likewise, when parents ask for the baptism of their infant, they are given an opportunity to reflect on their faith – the faith they will teach their child.

The time of enquiry

The catechetical process begins with the parents approaching the parish priest or the catechist(s) to ask how they can go about arranging for the baptism of their infant. Their first step is the formal request to be prepared for the baptism by submitting the form.

The time of catechesis

The parents are invited to some preparation sessions – an opportunity for them to go through the *Rite of Baptism* – giving them the chance to think about what they are asking for and helping them to understand the responsibility they are accepting to be the first teachers of their child in the ways of faith. The second step is the request for baptism; this might take place at a Sunday Mass with the presentation of the child to the community.

The time of prayerful preparation

This is the time when the parents and the parish community pray, in the bidding prayers, for the parents and the child who is to be baptised. It leads to the third step in the process: the celebration of the sacrament.

Mystagogia

During this time, the parents share with their children ways of living their faith by their example and by teaching them to pray.

First Communion

The children are prepared for their First Communion through the efforts of three groups of people: each child's own family, the catechists and the parish community as a whole. The members of these groups in the faith community, each with special experiences of what the Eucharist means to them, come together to pass on their faith and the Church's tradition on the Eucharist to the children in the parish.

The time of enquiry

The process may begin by seeing a notice in the parish bulletin to say that parents are invited to register their children (of a certain age or perhaps in a certain year in school) who can apply to be prepared for their First Communion. The first step in the process may be a presentation of the children at a Sunday Mass to enrol them in the programme.

The time of catechesis

The parents are invited to some catechetical sessions – a chance for them to learn about the programme that will be used so that they can help their children come to an understanding of the Eucharist. The children, too, will be invited to some catechetical sessions which will take them through the different parts of the Mass – something done in most of the First Communion programmes. The second step might be to invite the First Communion children and their families to a particular Sunday Mass where one part of the Mass is emphasised e.g. the Introductory Rites, the Liturgy of the Word etc. (At the Mass where the focus was on the Liturgy of the Word, the children might do the readings.) Most First Communion programmes guide the children through the Mass; and this is one way for the children to see in practice what they have been learning about in their programme.

The time of prayerful preparation

This is the time when, during the bidding prayers, the parents and the parish community pray for the children who are preparing to receive their First Communion. There may be a poster with the names of all the children or photos of them with a prayer request. The next step is the celebration of the Eucharist with the children.

Mystagogia

The children are sent forth to continue on their faith journey, bringing Christ out to the people they meet in faith, hope and love.

Confirmation

Parents have a variety of reasons for wanting their children to be confirmed. Some of them are worried that their children will not be able to get married in the Church if they are not confirmed.

This is true especially with teenagers, who may already have stopped coming to Mass regularly.

In the Archdiocese of Liverpool (and in many other places) children are confirmed before receiving their First Holy Communion. Instead of teachers, catechists and priests teaching children and parents about the sacraments, they help the parents to hand on their faith to their children, fulfilling the privileges and responsibilities expressed in the Rite of Baptism.[5]

The time of enquiry

The process may begin by seeing a notice in the parish bulletin to say that preparation for the sacrament of confirmation will begin at a certain time. Teenagers are invited to register for this preparation; if confirmation takes place at an earlier age, parents are invited to register their children in the programme. The first step in the process may be a Rite of Enrolment of the candidates at a Sunday Mass where the young people commit to taking this preparation seriously, participating in it with a generous heart.

The time of catechesis

The parents are invited to some catechetical sessions. For the children being prepared by their parents, this is the time when they will be prepared to prepare their children. Older children will be invited to some catechetical sessions which help them consider what it means to be a Christian; they will be prepared to renew their baptismal promises and will reflect on the Creed – what they believe and how they live. The second step might be for young people to make a formal request to celebrate the sacrament at a Sunday Mass.

The time of prayerful preparation

This is the time when, during the bidding prayers, the parents and the parish community pray for the youngsters preparing to be confirmed. There may be a poster with the names of all the youngsters or photos of them with a prayer request. The candidates themselves will also spend time in prayer and reflection. The next step is the celebration of the sacrament of confirmation.

Mystagogia

The youngsters are sent forth to continue on their faith journey, bringing Christ out to the people they meet in faith, hope and love.

Christian Initiation of Children of Catechetical Age (CICCA)

The Church gives us guidelines about what to include in our initiation of children of catechetical age in Part II of the *Rite of Christian Initiation of Adults* (the RCIA). This form of the rite is intended for children (7–14 years of age) who were not baptised as infants; they have attained the age of reason and we say they are of catechetical age. They follow the same process as the adults with only a few small differences. (See the chart in Chapter 7 on p.81.)

The CICCA tells us that these children should be prepared for and celebrate the three sacraments of initiation together. However, pastoral circumstances may suggest that they be prepared for confirmation and the Eucharist with the parish children to help them integrate into the parish community. There are not a lot of resources for the CICCA. One is *I call you friends, Book 3*;[6] another one is *The Christ we proclaim*,[7] which was published as an online book.

Sacramental preparation for people with learning disabilities

Efforts to find ways to help people with learning disabilities to know Jesus and to be more like him have led to a wide development of alternative and creative methods of catechesis which do not rely solely on the literate or verbal. Symbolic catechesis speaks from the heart. It is transformative of life and people's perception of the world – presenting an integrated and acculturated faith that unifies the diverse members of all cultures and all abilities in the community.

The process includes activities that interest, motivate and engage people, listening to scripture and breaking it open. It includes music, texture and colour which point us to different ways of mediating a faith formation entirely consonant with the richness and symbolism already apparent in our modes of prayer and worship. The activities you choose must have the potential to form a link or bridge to explore the theme of the session and to communicate the message of the scripture being used.[8]

Symbols of Faith is a programme of faith formation and sacramental preparation for people with learning disabilities. The process is the same as the one used in the RCIA, in keeping with Part II (the CICCA) and is adapted to accommodate the ability of the people being prepared using symbolic catechesis.[9]

Catechetical method

The very same catechetical method is used in most of the published materials used to prepare people for the sacraments of initiation. Remember how it works:

Remember how the disciples welcomed Jesus as he joined them on the Road to Emmaus. We also welcome people as we begin our sessions.
Jesus asked the disciples what had been going on; and he listened to them tell the story in their own words, from their own (human) experience.

In this first movement of this method, we are invited to a personal or faith experience related to the theme of the catechetical session.

Jesus opens the scriptures for the disciples – explaining how everything that had happened to him had been foretold.

In this second movement of the method, we are invited to turn to scripture passages and to the Tradition of the Church – God's story sheds light on our own story. In our catechetical sessions, we will include: Doctrine, Scripture, and Tradition, Liturgy and faith stories of our Catholic Church.

The disciples "got the message" and recognised Jesus when he blessed and broke the bread.

In this third movement of the method, we are invited to make a personal faith response.

Like the disciples, we want to go out to bring the Good News to those we meet – *the last movement.*

Catechetical formation

It is only through your personal encounter and experiences of God that you will be able to draw others into faith. If it is not personal for you, it will not be personal for them. If you do not know the person of Christ, you cannot tell others about him. If you don't live as a follower of Christ, you cannot show others how they can follow him.

Personal prayer is foundational to our spiritual lives. It is essential to our spiritual life.

The spiritual life of a catechist is characterised by

- a love of God – and God's holy people

- a practice of the faith in a spirit of faith, charity, hope, courage, and joy

- personal prayer and dedication to the evangelising mission of the Church

- a conviction of the truth of the Catholic faith and enthusiastically proclaiming it

- a devotion to Mary, the first disciple and the model of catechists, and to the Eucharist, the source of nourishment for catechists

- active participation in their local parish community.

From the *National Directory for Catechesis*, §54.B

Catechetical training courses

There are a good number of training programmes for catechists run in and by dioceses. There are also many good online courses available. For example, Maryvale Institute offers a course for anyone interested in developing his or her own faith for the sake of sharing it with others. The course includes practical aspects of catechesis as well as a solid foundation in key areas of theology and spirituality, so theory is put into practice all the way through the course.

Their Certificate in Catechesis is approved by the Congregation for the Clergy and is also offered with the authority of bishops from dioceses in England, Scotland and Ireland and around the world for the training of catechists for their dioceses. It is a two-year, part-time, distance-learning course. Course participants study at home in their own time following specially written coursebooks for each module of the course. For each module the student presents a piece of written work. On this particular course, there are three study days to attend during the year, at which students are introduced to the modules and a practical workshop – and each academic year ends with a retreat day. The course draws from the scriptures, the *Catechism of the Catholic Church* and selected documents of the Second Vatican Council as key reference texts and offers a balance of theology, spirituality and catechetical teaching skills. The programme begins with an introductory module on catechesis and on the foundations of faith; there are then modules covering these areas: Jesus Christ, the Church, Methodology, Scripture, Liturgy and the Sacraments and Prayer.

This is only one of many courses you can find online or at an accessible college. If you want to find training for yourself or for volunteers in your parish, you can find opportunities to do so.

Who is the catechist in the parish?

Catechists work in many different ways in parishes. They may be part of a team of people who are preparing others to celebrate the sacraments; they may be the team leader – coordinating the group; and they may be a parish coordinator, who has overall responsibility for all the parish catechetical programmes in the parish. Catechists may be the parents, they may be old or young, male or female, married or single; they may be paid parish workers and they may be volunteers. Finally, one should bear in mind that, as well as the lay catechists, there are a great number of religious men and women who carry out catechesis – and, of course, the priest is the catechist of catechists.

 POINTS TO REMEMBER

☑ The Rite of Christian Initiation of Adults is the model for all catechesis.

☑ The Church, in transmitting the faith, does not have a particular method nor any single method. In short, she assumes those methods which are not contrary to the Gospel and places them at its service (GDC 148).

☑ The three essential texts for catechists:
  • Scripture
  • The *Catechism of the Catholic Church*
  • The *General Directory for Catechesis.*

POINTS FOR PERSONAL REFLECTION OR GROUP DISCUSSION

▲ What have you learned in this chapter and why is it important for you to think about it?

▲ Which of the spiritual characteristics of a catechist best describes you? Why?

▲ Which characteristic provides the biggest challenge for you to work as a catechist? Why?

▲ Why are all these characteristics important as you seek to "echo Christ"?

Prayer for Catechists

Loving God, Creator of all things,
you call us to be in relationship with you and others.
Thank you for calling me to be a catechist,
  for the opportunity to share with others what you have given to me.
May all those with whom I share the gift of faith
  discover how you are present in all things.
May they come to know you, the one true God,
  and Jesus Christ, whom you have sent.
May the grace of the Holy Spirit guide my heart and lips,
  so that I may remain constant in loving and praising you.
May I be a witness to the Gospel and a minister of your truth.
May all my words and actions reflect your love. Amen.

Loyola Press (a Jesuit ministry)

ENDNOTES

[1] Thomas Groome, *Christian Religious Education – Sharing Our Story and Vision*, (Harper Collins Publishers, New York, 1980), 135-146.

[2] See Thomas Groome, about the movements, 207-228.

[3] James Dunning, *Echoing God's Word* (American Forum on the Catechumenate, Arlington, 1993), 20.

[4] Bernard Lonergan, *Insight*, (Philosophical Library, New York, 1957), and *Method in Theology*, (Darton, Longman and Todd, London, 1971) as quoted in James Dunning, *New Wine: New Wineskins, Pastoral Implications of the Rite of Christian Initiation of Adults*, (William Sadler, Chicago, New York, Los Angeles, 1981), 20-21.

[5] From a column by Jimmy Burns, "Confirmation then Communion in Liverpool", *The Tablet*, 29 January 2011.

[6] Diana Klein and Susanne Kowal (members of the CICCA Working Party of the Bishops' Conference of England and Wales), *I call you friends: Book 3* (McCrimmons, Great Wakering, Essex, 2009). This book is part of Living and Sharing Our Faith: A National Project for Catechesis and Religious Education.

[7] Diana Klein, *The Christ we proclaim*, online publication, (Westminster Diocese, London, 2010).

[8] From a Parish Practice article by Diana Klein, "When necessary, use words", *The Tablet*, 15 March 2014.

[9] Diana Klein, *Symbols of faith – faith formation and sacramental preparation for people with learning disabilities* (Redemptorist Publications, Chawton, Hampshire, 2015).

CHAPTER 7
CATECHESIS 2: *How liturgies can teach*

There is a renewed focus on the attractiveness of the Christian message in Pope Francis' two magisterial documents, *Evangelii Gaudium* and *Lumen Fidei*. In the latter, the Pope points out that the Church is a family, which must pass on the full store of its memories in a way that nothing is lost. How? Through the sacraments and celebrated in the Church's liturgy.

Christ is not a distant memory; he is a real presence in our lives today. There are occasions of particularly significant catechesis, such as baptisms, First Holy Communion, confirmations, marriages, funerals and so on. This chapter will review some of the key liturgies in our parishes. It will address some of the issues; it will tell you about good practice in parishes; and it will include ideas to help transform dull or difficult celebrations into life-giving ones.

Adult baptism

The Rite of Christian Initiation of Adults is a series of rituals and preparation that leads adults (and people from the age of 14) to baptism, confirmation and the Eucharist. The RCIA has two very important ramifications. The first is that the rituals are important and they need to be carried out and celebrated with all the richness and care that we can muster. The second is that we can gain some understanding of the process required for each section of the RCIA by examining the ritual to which it leads and by asking ourselves what words and actions are needed to make the celebration a true expression of what has happened in the lives of the catechumens up to then. The process must be designed and implemented in a way that will enable both the catechumens and the whole community to celebrate the rites honestly and fruitfully.

In the first stage of the RCIA, enquirers encounter and welcome Christ into their lives. When they are ready to proceed, they celebrate their first rite, asking to become catechumens. In some parishes, the rite is celebrated privately within the RCIA group; but the *Rite* (RCIA 43) says that it is desirable for the parish community to take an active part in the celebration. It is a catechetical opportunity that neither the enquirers nor the parish community should miss. The candidates are assembling publicly for the first time; they declare their intention to the Church and the Church accepts them as persons who intend to become its members (RCIA 41). There follows a good example of how one parish celebrated the rite.

The priest and the catechists asked the enquirers to meet at the main door of the church before Mass began, equipped with a baseball bat. The Mass began as normal and continued up to the "Amen" following the Collect. At this point, the enquirers banged on the church door with the bat and the priest asked the server (who had been primed and given a handheld microphone) to go to the door and to report back. The altar server did this and said, "There are some people here who want to join the Church." The priest asked the server to invite them all inside and he asked them one by one to introduce themselves, and to state what they were asking of God's Church. The replies were various and moving. Some said they wanted to join the Church, to be part of that community, some said they wanted to become a Catholic and others said they wanted to know more about Jesus.

The priest then invited them all to come and stand at the front of the church standing before the altar facing the assembly, each with their sponsor standing behind them. This was followed by the candidates' first acceptance of the Gospel, the affirmation by the sponsors and assembly and the signing of the candidates with the cross as the ritual book indicates. The celebrant signed the candidates on their foreheads as a sign that Christ now strengthened them with a sign of his love; the sponsors signed the other senses, ears (that they would hear the voice of God), the eyes (that they would see the glory of God), the lips (that they would respond to the word of God), the breast (that Christ might dwell there) and the shoulders (that they might bear the gentle yoke of Christ) (RCIA 54-56).[1]

The rite concludes with prayer and the invitation to listen to the word of God and the Mass continues with the offertory procession.

The RCIA: stages and steps along the way

Period of Evangelisation and Pre-catechumenate: a time, of no fixed duration or structure, for enquiry and introduction to Gospel values, an opportunity for the beginnings of faith, leading to:

First step: Acceptance into the Order of Catechumens: this is the first liturgical rite, which marks the beginning of the catechumenate proper, as the enquirers express and the Church accepts their intention to respond to God's call to follow the way of Christ – and they become the catechumens.

Period of the Catechumenate: the time for the nurturing and growth of the catechumens' faith and conversion to God. Minor rites included in this period are the celebrations of the word, and prayers of exorcism and blessing are meant to assist the process. This leads to:

Second step: Election or Enrolment of Names: this is the second liturgical rite, usually celebrated on the First Sunday of Lent, when the Church formally ratifies the catechumens' readiness for the sacraments of initiation and the catechumens, who are now the elect, express their desire for the sacraments.

Period of Purification and Enlightenment: usually the Lenten season preceding the celebration of initiation at the Easter Vigil; it is a time of reflection, centred on conversion, marked by celebration of the scrutinies and presentations and of the preparation rites on Holy Saturday. This leads to:

Third step: Celebration of the Sacraments of Initiation: this is the liturgical rite, usually integrated into the Easter Vigil by which the elect are initiated through baptism, confirmation, and the Eucharist.

Period of Post-baptismal Catechesis or Mystagogy: this is the time, usually the Easter season, following the celebration of initiation, during which the newly initiated experience being fully part of the Christian community by means of pertinent catechesis and particularly by participation with all the faithful in the Sunday Eucharistic celebration. This leads to the rest of their lives lived in faith, hope and charity.

Baptism of children of catechetical age

Children from age 7–14 are (or should be) prepared for the sacraments of baptism, confirmation and the Eucharist by following Part II of the Rite of Christian Initiation of Adults: the Christian Initiation of Children of Catechetical Age (the CICCA). They come asking to become Catholic. They may have relatives or friends who go to church, they may have come to church for a baptism, a wedding or a funeral – or, they may already be coming to Mass, and they want to belong.

There are a growing number of these older children who are coming to the Church asking for baptism and many parishes don't know what to do with them. Some get them to join the First Holy Communion group and baptise them just before they receive Communion. If they are a little older, some parishes get them to join the confirmation group; but the fact is that the Church has given us the CICCA and we should be following the rich rituals in it.

Like the RCIA, it is important for the children to experience being part of the faith community; this is often done by inviting some of their peers to accompany them as they follow through their journey of faith and prepare to celebrate the sacraments of initiation. During their preparation, they will come to know and desire to follow Christ; they will listen to him speaking to them in scripture; they will spend time learning how to pray and will discover how to live by faith.

Since the Church's life is apostolic, the children and their families might be encouraged to work with others in the parish outreach to the poor. A keen social conscience is normally found in children of this age. To join with others of their own age group in activities – such as packing food parcels for the elderly and poor at Christmas, preparing sandwiches for homeless people, engaging in fundraising for the Catholic charity Cafod or other Catholic charities, or local hospices or parish projects abroad – helps them not only to make new friends but gives a sense of purpose to their lives.[2]

The CICCA process (for older children)

Period of Evangelisation and Pre-catechumenate: a time, of no fixed duration or structure, for enquiry and introduction to Gospel values, an opportunity for the beginnings of faith, leading to:

First step: Acceptance into the Order of Catechumens: this marks the beginning of the catechumenate proper, as the children say they want to respond to God's call to follow Jesus.

Period of the Catechumenate: in duration this will correspond to the progress of the child; celebrations of the word and prayers of exorcism and blessing assist the process. It leads to:

Second step: the Scrutiny: the second step in the Christian initiation of these older children is the celebration of a scrutiny or Penitential Rite. (Though there are many similarities in the journey, there are some obvious differences because we need to adapt things to meet the particular spiritual needs that young people have. One of the differences is that the Rite of Election is not included for children.)

Period of Purification and Enlightenment: this is the time immediately preceding the elects' initiation, preceding the celebration of this initiation at the Easter Vigil; it is a time of reflection, intensely centred on conversion, marked by the preparation rites on Holy Saturday. This leads to:

Third step: Celebration of the Sacraments of Initiation: this is the liturgical rite, usually integrated into the Easter Vigil, by which the elect are initiated through baptism, confirmation, and the Eucharist.

Period of Post-baptismal Catechesis or Mystagogy: this is the time, usually the Easter season, following the celebration of initiation, during which the newly initiated experience being fully a part of the Christian community by means of pertinent catechesis and particularly by participation with all the faithful in the Sunday Eucharistic celebration.

Infant baptism

The Rite of Infant Baptism is the rite used for infants and children up to seven years of age. Their baptisms sometimes take place in a cold dark church on a Sunday afternoon with no music and nobody present from the members of the parish community where they are being baptised. What's more, what happens during the baptism is not well understood by the family and friends who come to the baptism.

Many parishes have wrestled with this dilemma and a number of different solutions have been proposed. One is to have most or all baptisms during Sunday masses, when families may meet other members of their parish community for the first time. Another option is for a parish to celebrate its baptisms only once a month, with two or more families in attendance at a special baptism liturgy (including music). Yet another option is the selection and formation of a baptism team to meet with families ahead of the baptism, explaining the rite to them and welcoming them into the parish community. These can also help families to be involved in the sacrament, by reading the word of God and the intercessions.

As part of this effort, one parish made a film of a re-enacted baptism in their church. They included stopping-points in the film with an explanation of the signs and symbols of the sacrament – and the deeper significance of baptism. They planned the film so that it could be paused and the parents invited into discussion during the preparation session. For example, after the greeting outside the church or in the porch, the film could be paused and the parents could be asked what they are asking for. They are asked why they have chosen the name they have given their child and why we make the sign of the cross. During this pause, there could also be a reflection on what it means to belong to Christ.

The film then shows how all move into the nave of the church to listen to the reading of scripture. People move from place to place in the church during the Rite of Baptism to show how we are on a journey of faith. There is another stopping-point here, where the parents can be asked to think about what God might be saying through the readings.

They then move to the baptismal font. Parents find it very powerful to reflect on how the waters of baptism bring their child to new life – and how being anointed with chrism will help the child be more like Christ and to take on his mission. The baptism concludes with the family and friends moving to the altar, where this child will eventually receive Holy Communion; and they say the Lord's Prayer – the prayer of our Christian family, a family this child now belongs to.

With more and more people having access to modern technology, parishes can tailor-make their own baptism preparation programmes; they do not have to be dependent on a published programme which may not suit them. Seeing a baptism in a place you are familiar with and with the priest who will be baptising your child makes this film a very powerful catechetical tool.[3]

The parents can receive a copy of the DVD to take home and watch again prior to the baptism. They might invite friends and relatives who will be at the baptism to come and watch it with them to help them understand the importance of this event for them and their child.

The Rite of Infant Baptism during Mass	And, outside of Mass
• The welcoming may have taken place separately – e.g. during one of the preparation sessions; or it can take place at the door at the start of Mass	Reception of the child, parents and godparents at the church door • After the dialogue, the priest welcomes the child and claims him/her for Christ by marking the cross on the child's head
• The readings used in the Mass replace the scripture readings normally used in baptism	The Rite continues in the nave of the church with an invitation to the celebration of the word of God
• The whole community profess their faith in place of the Creed during Mass	• A minister reads the first reading and may sing the psalm • The Gospel is read; there may be a homily
• The Mass continues with the baptism. The celebrant invites the family to the font for the baptism, anointing, clothing, presentation of candle and Ephphetha	• The bidding prayers are said by family members • The Preparatory Rite now follows with: • The prayer of exorcism and anointing before baptism with the oil of catechumens
• Bidding prayers will be the ones used for the Mass; although they are likely to include the newly baptised child and his/her family	The celebration of baptism • Blessing of the water • Profession of faith and renunciation of sin • Baptism
• Mother, father and community are blessed at the end of Mass.	• Anointing after baptism with chrism • Clothing with the white garment • Presentation of the candle • Ephphetha
	Next, there is a procession to the altar – where the parents will lead their child/children to the Eucharist in time • There, they say the Lord's Prayer on behalf of the baby – who is now part of the Christian family • They are blessed.

First Holy Communion

First Communion is a very special event in a family's life – and parents (even non-practising ones) will do whatever it takes to make sure their child is prepared for the big day. The event stirs up memories in parents of the day they first received Communion – and they want their children to have a similar experience. Sadly, though, this is not so easy for the many children who rarely come to Mass on Sunday – and, since nearly all preparatory programmes are based on what happens in the Mass, it makes it difficult for children to make sense of the preparation.

An excellent programme called *Do This in Memory* is in place in many parishes in Ireland. It is a resource that parishes use to support both parents and children alike as they prepare for First Communion. Participants are invited to attend a monthly Sunday Mass through the school year, which is particularly geared for them. Newsletters (for the parents) and worksheets (for the children) create links between the monthly Masses, and families are encouraged to create a sacred space at home, in which the themes of the sacred seasons can be reflected. At the end of the year, the children and parents who have participated feel more at home in their church, and are more prepared to be involved in the Sunday liturgy, more part of the parish life.[4]

A welcome development in recent years is the provision of catechetical support in the parish, where the children meet with catechists and helpers throughout the time of preparation and there are three or four parents' meetings during the programme. Since the aim of the First Communion programmes is to teach the children about the Mass, there can be a celebration Mass for them at one of the Sunday masses four times during the programme: the first two (celebrating the Introductory Rites and the Liturgy of the Word) take place prior to First Communion (which celebrates the Liturgy of the Eucharist) and the last one takes place after the children have received their First Communion. This one can be a sending forth Mass (to celebrate the Concluding Rites of the Mass).

For example, in one parish, they celebrate the Introductory Rites of the Mass by presenting the children to the parish community. The children are invited then to come forward with a parent (who has brought the child's baptismal candle). They stand facing the congregation where the priest and the altar servers light all the candles. The priest tells the children that they were given a lighted candle on the day they were baptised; and, on that day, they were told:

"You have been enlightened by Christ. Walk always as children of the light." He adds that maybe they were too small to understand it then; and he invites the parents to hand the baptismal candles to their children again, now saying, as they do: "Receive the light of Christ and bring it to everyone you meet."

This enables the children to make the link between receiving Jesus in the Eucharist and taking him out to those they meet. It also enables the priest to make the link between baptism and First Communion. This is the reason that girls wear white dresses for their First Communion – although, somehow, that symbolism has got lost in the elaborate and expensive dresses the girls are now wearing – and, for some reason, the symbolism doesn't extend at all to the boys!

In some parishes, they brace themselves for the extravagant parties and shows of excess as First Communion season comes upon them. One priest reported that a seven-year-old girl was transported to church in a Cinderella coach for her First Communion. Another girl arrived at church with a dog dressed in an identical dress to her own. And, what's more, a few years ago, there was a girl who wore a tiara in church and, when she received the Host for the first time, the tiara lit up.[5]

One mother complained after her daughter received First Communion, saying that there is a long way to go if we are to help our children celebrate this special event in their lives with a sense of the importance and depth of the sacrament. Her solution to the problem would be to teach the children a repertoire of traditional hymns as part of their preparation. She thinks it would be a way of exposing children to a kind of piety that their formation might otherwise lack – and that this would help them receive the sacrament with understanding, awe and mystery.[6]

Some would make the point that many of the traditional hymns this mum suggests were written in the context of static devotion rather than an active participatory liturgy. We have now a new generation of hymns that reflects a post-conciliar understanding of what we do at Mass.[7]

The point is that, if we are to reach the catechetical potential of preparation and celebration of First Communion, anything we can do to help parents and children to want to come to Mass regularly, to learn more about the Mass, how it developed, how it is celebrated and what Holy Communion means, is

essential. This approach is built on the belief that children grow in faith best when their parents and the parish community accompany them on their faith journey.

Confirmation

Young people in their thousands celebrate the sacrament of confirmation each year, ranging in age from birth to fifteen years of age. Some eight-year-olds will be confirmed and receive their First Communion; the others will have received First Communion years before and are being confirmed as teenagers – all depending on whether they are in the Eastern or Western Church and on their diocese.

In the early Church, adults seeking to become Christians would be immersed in water by presbyters or deacons at the Easter Vigil; they would then go to the bishop, who would lay his hands on them and anoint them and they would then receive the Eucharist. As Christianity grew, bishops could not always be present for baptisms. The Eastern Church continued to confirm immediately after baptism, sacrificing the bishop's personal involvement; but, in the West, the bishops reserved the "anointings" after baptism to themselves, wanting to keep a role in the ritual of initiation (thereby sacrificing the immediacy of confirmation). The bishop, so to speak, confirms the baptism performed earlier by the priest or deacon.

The Eastern Churches give Holy Communion immediately, even to newly baptised infants; but from the Council of Trent on, the Latin Church reserved admission to Holy Communion to those who had attained the age of reason. In fact, children's catechesis regularly began around the age of seven, when confirmation could be administered, and culminated with First Communion around the age of eleven or twelve. Over time, a feeling that catechesis was necessary also for confirmation led to the age of confirmation creeping up to join that of First Communion, though officially confirmation was still located at the age of discretion, that is, seven.

It is important to remember this, because when Pius X brought the age of First Communion down to the age of seven in 1910, he was taking it to where confirmation officially was. However, since confirmation was in practice celebrated later, the result of his reform was that First Communion began to take place long before confirmation – and this meant that the pattern of initiation from the time of the early Church was broken and confirmation and First Communion were reversed.[8]

This link between baptism and confirmation still exists; and the Church still teaches that the bishop confirms the baptism performed earlier by the priest. For example, the Rite of Confirmation says that it is desirable that the godparent at baptism, if available, should be the sponsor at confirmation (although they do not exclude the option of choosing a special sponsor for confirmation).[9] The Introduction to the Rite tells us that confirmation strengthens and confirms what happens in baptism – completing the grace of baptism. This is why the renewal of baptismal promises takes place preceding the reception of the sacrament of confirmation.

In some parishes, the confirmandi carry their baptismal candles in procession at the beginning of their confirmation Mass. Alternatively, some light their baptismal candle from the paschal candle prior to renewing their baptismal promises. In some parishes, all the confirmandi (male and female) dress in a white baptismal robe; in others, there is a sprinkling rite with liberal amounts of water (or procession to the font) that takes place during the Introductory Rites.

Any way to bind baptism and confirmation together in the liturgy is helpful – and offers a catechetical opportunity to remind all those present of the link between the two sacraments.

The Rite of Confirmation during Mass	And, outside of Mass
• Gathering Rites and Liturgy of the Word (readings of the day on Sundays or solemnities)	• Gathering Rites and Liturgy of the Word (readings of the day on Sundays or solemnities)
• The Rite of Confirmation itself begins after the Gospel with the presentation of the candidates to the bishop	• The Rite of Confirmation begins after the Gospel with the presentation of the candidates to the bishop
• Homily follows	• Homily follows
• The candidates are invited to renew their baptismal promises	• The candidates are invited to renew their baptismal promises
• The bishop lays hands on the candidates	• The bishop lays hands on the candidates
• The candidates are anointed with chrism	• The candidates are anointed with chrism
• General intercessions	• General intercessions
• Mass then continues with the Liturgy of the Eucharist and finishes as usual with the Rite of Dismissal.	• (There is no Liturgy of the Eucharist) • Rite of Dismissal.

The sacrament of reconciliation

Catholics do not go to confession frequently (or even regularly) as once was the case. Read this story about how one priest was able to challenge a penitent:

A man committed adultery. He went to confession on Saturday morning; and, for his penance, he was told to say three Hail Marys. The following Saturday, he went to confession again; he told the priest he didn't think he'd heard him properly the week before. This time he was told to say five decades of the rosary. This continued on the third Saturday. The man was convinced that the priest hadn't understood the seriousness of his sin. This time, he was told to say all twenty decades of the rosary every day for a week – not for committing adultery, but for not believing in the mercy and unconditional love of God.

Many people talk about the need to confess their sins; but they express feelings of dissatisfaction – a feeling that things are not as they should be with this sacrament, saying it does not feel as beneficial, as positive an experience, as it should. Their problems stem from a failure really to believe in the mercy and unconditional love of God. They don't believe that, in this sacrament, we encounter the living God, that there is another present beside priest and penitent, that Christ is speaking to them through the priest. The fact that the Church now talks about "celebrating the Sacrament of Reconciliation" in contrast to "going to confession" should speak volumes; but for these people, it doesn't do what it says on the tin.

In an effort to help people shift in their understanding of this sacrament, many parishes have services of reconciliation each year in Lent and in Advent.

They are communal services with individual private confessions. Confession is an intimate experience; but the Catholic Church maintains that there is a social aspect to sin – and that is why we celebrate the sacrament together as a community. Our sins not only affect our relationship with God; our sin also alienates us from other people and from the Church.

One parish used the scripture story of the man born blind for one of these services (John 9:1-12). This man's life changed completely when he was healed; he saw things from a completely new perspective. The homily that followed at this service invited people to see how they needed to change. For the examination of conscience, a prayer was read and people responded with a sung response, the Taizé chant, "O Lord, hear my prayer". The prayers expressed the desire for good to be stirred up within us in order that we might see like the man born blind, whose sight was restored. They asked for grace that opens our eyes and hearts to see and love those in need. And, aware of our desire to imitate Christ's love and patience in our own lives, the prayer invites us to consider when we have not been tolerant of one another, of poor and homeless people, of refugees, or of elderly people, of our own family members and workmates.[10]

Since music can help to set a reflective and prayerful tone, the parish used Jesse Manibusan's hymn, "Open my eyes Lord, let me see your face". One aim of this liturgy was to give people the chance to reflect on their own life experience, to listen to the scripture, to connect what we believe with how we live. The ultimate aim, of course, is to be reminded of the mercy and unconditional love of God.

The structure of a penitential service

The community gathers around a suitable focal point. The structure will be:

- a Gathering Rite (probably with an opening hymn)

- opening prayers

- a Liturgy of the Word with an appropriate choice of scripture readings followed by

- a homily and an examination of conscience

- a litany

- individual confession (when people go one at a time to a priest)

- prayer, blessing and dismissal.

Marriage

From the perspective of a priest struggling to survive working in a Catholic parish, wedding ceremonies provide one of the hardest challenges. The priest in a small parish with just a few marriages in a year can probably preside relatively easily, showing forbearance and patience. However, clergy with large numbers of weddings to prepare and preside over, who nevertheless do these with kindness, are to be highly commended. Many priests would choose to preside at many funerals in preference to one wedding, such are the difficulties they can pose.

One of the main problems from a presider's point of view is that couples preparing for marriage are members of the population cohort least in contact with church and parish life. Priests often see this when the format of the liturgy is being prepared and a booklet is being put together. Couples often have only the sketchiest idea of what comes where in the Mass, and are tempted to copy other booklets, repeating mistakes frequently found in these. Websites such as www.gettingmarried.ie are recommended by priests to couples to help them prepare wedding booklets that follow the recognised order of service and use the words the Church provides, instead of prayers devised by couples themselves.

The lack of familiarity with church services is often seen when the bridal party at the top of the church (and their friends and contemporaries) do not know when to stand, sit or kneel, or respond to even the simplest prayers of the Mass. A presider needs great patience then to perform effectively as a wedding presider. The following suggestions may help him:

- If you are solemnising a wedding ceremony, make sure you are in good form, by celebrating only that Mass on that day, and arriving in the church rested and calm.

- A rehearsal of the words of the ceremony with the couple and their two witnesses may help put them at ease; often more extravagant rehearsals with large numbers of people in attendance only add to the nervousness of everyone.

- Ask couples to choose people who are ministers of the Word to read for their wedding; if these cannot be found, suggest that the temporary readers practise their readings at the ambo in advance of the ceremony. Those who read the intercessions should do likewise.

- If there is tension in the church as the Mass begins, sometimes an early "sign of peace" helps break the ice. Presiders use this before Mass begins by asking people to cross to the other side of the aisle and make sure other guests feel welcome. This often helps put everyone at ease.

- Presiders at wedding ceremonies have to take more care than usual to lead the community into prayerfulness. Before ministerial prayers such as the Collect (Opening Prayer), they must remind the congregation that is the moment when they ask God to look after the couple about to marry.

- The homily at the Wedding Mass should be firmly rooted in the word of God. Sometimes the presider might choose the Gospel on which he is working for the following Sunday as the basis for the wedding homily, if he can easily adapt the themes for the

Sunday homily to the wedding. "Stock" wedding sermons should be avoided if possible.

• The presider has to give a careful instruction at Communion time about who may receive. Invite those who do not attend Mass but wish to be part of the liturgy to come for a blessing; the presider explains how this is signified.

• Couples who are not regular participants in church life, or couples where one is a non-Roman Catholic Christian, should be encouraged to celebrate the wedding service without Mass (consisting of the Liturgy of the Word, Liturgy of Marriage, intercessions, Our Father and blessings). See the table below.

An important part of the preparation will include the planning for the liturgy of the wedding. The couple may need help to choose Christian music; if they want something else, some presiders ask to see the lyrics in advance of the liturgy to make sure that all is as it should be. The celebration of self-giving and personal relationship is now expressed in modern liturgies – and the readings should be chosen accordingly. When we are planning the liturgy with the couple, we have an ideal opportunity to express our *belief* that the love, concern and self-giving that each has for the other expresses Christ's love for each of them.

The Rite of Marriage during the Mass	And, outside of Mass
• The Gathering Rite and welcome	• The Gathering Rite and welcome
• The Liturgy of the Word	• The Liturgy of the Word
• The Rite of Marriage, followed by:	• The Rite of Marriage, followed by:
• The Prayer of the Faithful, which will be focused on the couple, their family, any absent or deceased friends or family	• The Prayer of the Faithful, which will be focused on the couple, their family, any absent or deceased friends or family
• The Liturgy of the Eucharist	• (There is no Liturgy of the Eucharist)
• The Concluding Rites	• The Lord's Prayer
• The signing of the register.	• A marriage nuptial blessing
	• The Concluding Rites
	• The signing of the register.

Funerals

At least one thing every family in the whole world shares: they will find themselves at some time having to organise a funeral for one they love dearly. It will never be easy, no matter what the circumstances. The Church has a most poignant role at the end of life, although a priest can often be overstretched in dealing with the bereaved.

The Diocese of Cork & Ross in Ireland took some steps to involve parishioners in an official accompanying role in the funeral liturgies. It was presented as a continuation of the "ministry of consolation" to which all the baptised are called. These laypeople were to help families prepare the funeral rites, select appropriate readings, prepare intercessions and decide on how the bereaved should participate in the funeral rites. Some members of the Pastoral Teams for Funerals, as these ministers were called, were also formed and commissioned to preside at funeral services, including the Vigil for the Deceased (and rosary), the Transfer of the Body to the church and committal services.[11]

Liverpool followed in 2012: they were the first diocese in England and Wales formally to commission laypeople to conduct funeral services. The then Archbishop Patrick Kelly said that he was sometimes being asked why people "had to wait so long for a funeral to be celebrated in one of our churches".[12] It had become apparent that the number of funerals priests were being asked to conduct and the subsequent delays for families was an area of real concern so they looked at the *Order of Christian Funerals* (OCF).[13]

It envisages that a layperson may lead parts of the funeral rites since the celebration of a Requiem Mass may not, for a myriad of reasons, be the most appropriate means of celebrating the funeral of a particular individual. The OCF gives a diversity of rites involving various people. There are three main stages: a Prayer Vigil, usually the evening before the funeral; the Funeral Liturgy, which may be a Mass or a Liturgy of the Word; and the Committal at the cemetery or crematorium.

Both in Cork and in Liverpool, those chosen for this ministry undergo a course in formation. Their preparation is crucial; they must be well versed in the human experience and understanding of the stages of bereavement, and in the collaborative approach to ministering to the bereaved so that their presence will be a positive assistance to the mourners at such a delicate time of their lives.

Archbishop Kelly said this development in Liverpool was an opportunity to recognise what the funeral liturgy is all about. This is urgent among those who rarely come to Mass.

The Rite of Funerals during Mass	And, outside Mass
• A family member may say a few words before Mass begins and mementoes of the deceased's life may be placed near the coffin	• The Gathering Rite and welcome
• The Gathering Rite follows, with Penitential Rite and Collect	• The Liturgy of the Word, including homily and the Prayer of the Faithful (focused on the deceased, their family, any absent or deceased friends or family)
• The Liturgy of the Word, including homily and the Prayer of the Faithful (focused on the deceased, their family, any absent or deceased friends or family)	• (There is no Liturgy of the Eucharist)
• The Liturgy of the Eucharist	• The Lord's Prayer
• The Final Commendation and the Farewell Chant	• A family member may give a eulogy
• The Final Prayer.	• The Final Commendation and the Farewell Chant
	• The Final Prayer.

POINTS FOR PERSONAL REFLECTION OR GROUP DISCUSSION

Rituals are an important part of life and they need to be carried out and celebrated with all the richness and care that we can muster – and the catechetical opportunities they offer should be fully tapped.

Think of the catechetical opportunities you read about in this chapter. Reflect on them and what you may have learned from hearing about them

 in baptisms for adults and infants

 in First Communion masses

 in confirmation masses

 in reconciliation liturgies

 in weddings

 in funerals

When the enquirers in an RCIA group are asked what they want of the Church, some say they want to join the Church, to be part of our community. Think about what it was that makes them want to be part of our Church.

How would you reply to someone who asks you what makes you want to be part of the Church?

Think about a memorable celebration of one of the sacraments for you and explore why you found it memorable. Spend some time in prayer with your memory.

 *Prayer*

*Gracious and loving God, you satisfy our need
to encounter you in our liturgical celebrations.
Through these liturgies, you continue to quench
our thirst for your presence in our lives,
for your comfort in times of loss, for your
strength in times of weakness
and for your power in times of uncertainty.
We ask you to continue to be with us
on our journey through life –
always aware of your presence.
We ask this in the name of Christ our Lord
and the power of the Holy Spirit. Amen.*

ENDNOTES

[1] This idea for the Acceptance into the Order of Catechumens came from a Parish Practice article by James Leachman, "Knocking at the front door" in the issue of *The Tablet*, 1 December 2007.

[2] Edit of a Parish Practice article by Diana Klein, "Children called to holiness", *The Tablet*, 13 March 2010.

[3] Idea for this film came from a Parish Practice article by Fr Ulick Loring, "Home Truths", which appeared in *The Tablet*, 12 May 2012.

[4] Idea from an article by Bernard Cotter, "All together now", *The Tablet*, 20 June 2009.

[5] Extracts from a feature article by Sarah MacDonald and Isabel de Bertodano, "First Communion follies", *The Tablet*, 9 May 2009.

[6] Extracts from a Parish Practice article by Melanie McDonagh, "Bread of heaven", *The Tablet*, 15 August 2015.

[7] Quote from Paul Inwood in response to Melanie McDonagh's article above. Letter to *The Tablet*, 22 August 2015.

[8] From a Parish Practice article by Diana Klein, "Age of initiation", *The Tablet*, 12 February 2011.

[9] *The Rite of Confirmation*, Introduction 5; see also Canon 893 §2.

[10] Partially edited version of "Eyes wide open", Parish Practice article by Diana Klein, *The Tablet*, 2 March 2013.

[11] Based on a Parish Practice article by Bernard Cotter, "Consolation at a time of loss", *The Tablet*, 14 May 2011.

[12] Based on an article by Archbishop Patrick Kelly, "In lay hands", *The Tablet*, 1 September 2012.

[13] *Order of Christian Funerals* (1991), General Introduction #14.

CHAPTER 8

COMMUNICATION: *It's more than good microphones*

It's said that rather than the Church having a message, the message has a church. That message is the Good News of Jesus' life and teachings, his death and resurrection, and our Church was founded to make this news known. Communication is vital if we are to succeed in this task, and that involves more than installing good microphones – though without these, little is communicated except noise.

Communication is an aspect of the liturgy, helped by the ministry of good ministers of the Word and effective preachers. But equally importantly, communication is a vital aspect of parish life, seen in church newsletters, websites, parish magazines – and in honest speaking and listening within the parish. Communicating the Good News also involves making sure church buildings are welcoming places, with care taken of people with special needs, with whom communication is always more than just words.

Start with the microphones

While some pastors approach a church building hoping to improve its art and architecture, pastoral practitioners in parishes realise that the comfort and safety of those who attend church services means that three qualities of a church top every list: heat, light and sound. It doesn't matter how long or short a service, if the people in the pews are frozen, they won't get much from it. Dimly lit churches also take from the value of any liturgy, but churches where the sound system doesn't work properly can cause the most frustration of all.

It can be hard for those of us who work in parishes to keep up with developments in sound systems and sound technology. But often a parish will have a resident whose livelihood is tied up with being heard – an entertainer or band member who uses mobile sound systems, or a funeral director who provides mobile microphones for cemetery services, or indeed a technician whose day-job involves ensuring people are heard. The advice of such a person can be sought when a review of the church's sound system is undertaken, prior to making contact with a commercial firm. The local expert's advice will be crucial, particularly if he is a regular attender of church services, as this person experiences the church when it is full for weekend services, while often the commercial firm adjusts sound levels for the empty church of a weekday. Upgrading of equipment will also be necessary from time to time, though shopping around and getting three tenders before hiring a firm will usually ensure the (often cash-strapped) parish will get the best value going. The advice of a trusted parishioner-expert will be an important part of this process, also.

Even simple things need to be communicated properly

Even simple things in a church can fall victim to miscommunication. Take, for example, the priest who finds himself stuck for an idea for a Sunday homily, who then invites the congregation to reflect on one of the statues in the sanctuary: "My dear people," he might begin, "look at the beautiful image on the right. Behold the motherly face, the tender, loving eyes. See how lovingly she looks upon her child. Feel her love as it descends equally upon each of you…"

This fictional priest then continues in like mode. His homily on the image of Mary is missing its target, however: he has invited the congregation to look to the right – without clarifying whose right is in question. To *his* right as he looks at the congregation is the Marian statue. But the whole congregation is looking to *its* right, as they have been asked to do, at the bearded and not very tender-looking face of St Vincent de Paul…

It's a basic error of communication that regularly occurs in churches, where priests and people see things from (literally) different perspectives.
The priest who talks about the "back door" of the church is in similar territory. People imagine he is talking about some small door from the sacristy to the wilderness behind the church building. In his own mind, however, he is alluding to what people consider to be the main door of their church.

If communication is to be effective, one has to understand how another looks on things, how the other sees the world. Communication requires understanding of the other's standpoint, even in as simple a matter as where the other perceives the right and left side to be. If a priest has not understood this basic difference of viewpoint, communication on more significant matters offers little chance of success.[1]

Sometimes use words…

"Preach the Gospel always and if necessary use words." This phrase is attributed to St Francis of Assisi. It conveys well the non-verbal as well as verbal aspects of communication. Sometimes words must be used to communicate, in the liturgy and outside of it. The priest is supposed to be the principal wordsmith of the parish community, though others can easily surpass him in communication skills. His principal and most frequent exercise of communication will be his weekly homily, a central part of the Mass on Sundays and holy days. Writing a sermon that is relevant and insightful is one of a priest's greatest challenges.

The priest preparing a Sunday homily is advised to start on Sunday, after Mass, by picking up the following Sunday's missalette containing the Mass readings. This can stay in his pocket for the week, with some time spent in prayer each day, poring over these words, looking for inspiration to see what the Lord might want preached. Always, the bottom-line question of each Sunday's homily preparation remains the same: where is the Good News here?

From time to time a group of parishioners may participate in a *Lectio Divina* group in the parish, perhaps for Advent or Lent. This can be a help to the priest with his homily preparation: it's remarkable how differently people will view the same words, reflecting their life experiences.

It's useful for preachers to meet each other too. Priests (and deacons) can set aside a day a month to discuss and pray the word of God. In preparation, each would research the readings they set out to probe at their meeting, checking out commentaries, biblical dictionaries and concordances. It's not that the pulpit is the place for minute exegesis, but without a deep understanding of the text being preached from, effective preaching is impossible.

For many priests, Saturday is writing day, before the evening Mass. In some cases, the homily gets written down, word for word, though others prefer to write headings. Most priests try to memorise the main points of the homily, though it always helps to know that there's a script nearby. Then, neither crying child nor mobile phone can come between the preacher and his task.

Pope Francis encourages brevity in the homily; but there is no hard and fast rule. Some would say five minutes is a good length for a homily. Once priests get a reputation for excessive length, however, people switch off when such priests appear on the altar. A reputation for relative brevity gives one a better chance of being listened to.

A period of silence after a homily is also useful. Some priests will move back to the presider's chair at this stage, to emphasise the reflective character of the moment.

There is an opportunity later in the Mass to give a summary of the homily. After Communion and the notices, one can give a parting word – a brief synopsis of the homily. Taking the missalette with the readings home can also be recommended to the assembly, with the words that have provided the springboard for the homily pointed out.

The reactions of those who have listened are helpful too. It is useful to the preacher to be at the church entrance as people leave – accepting compliments graciously but taking critical comments too. Those who listen carefully to preachers help them stay in line with what the Church would want preached. Sometimes a comment received at the church door can cause a homily for a later Mass to be nuanced.

A more formal means of assessing homilies would be to invite members of a congregation to a meeting, at least occasionally. In advance, a summary of each homily preached in the previous month could be distributed, and perhaps these might also be included in the parish newsletter and website, which might help entice more parishioners to such a meeting. This gathering would copper-fasten parishioners' part in the ministry of the Word, as well as providing the preacher with the voice of the people.[2]

For people in pastoral ministry, there are other preaching moments. Funerals come regularly and often unexpectedly in parish life. The funeral liturgy takes place after a couple of conversations with the bereaved, whose words usually suggest readings and consequent homily thoughts. Weddings are less unexpected, but can prove difficult for preaching. For all the work of preparation that goes into them, consideration of appropriate readings from the word of God seem to come at the bottom of some couples' lists, which makes the preacher's task all the harder. Sometimes the celebrant can ask the couple to leave the choice of Gospel up to him, and if it seems suitable the Sunday Gospel can be read and the Sunday homily adapted for the occasion.

Many other events turn up that demand a homily too – including holy days of obligation, although these latter turn up regularly enough for the preacher to carry the germ of an idea from one year to the next.[3] Many priests take the opportunity to share a few words about dying and eternal life in November at masses for the dead. Indeed a homily, or at least a few thoughts at daily Mass is recommended during the more significant liturgical seasons: Lent and Easter, Advent and Christmas.

Others communicate at Mass, too

The priest-celebrant is not the sole communicator at masses, of course. The ministers of the Word, or readers, play an important role in reading the word of God, as do deacons, who also read the Gospel on occasion, and may preach. On some occasions, a lay member of the congregation can act as a commentator, steering the assembly through a unique liturgy (e.g. an ordination or profession, or the liturgies of the Easter Triduum). Laypeople also occasionally read a reflection at Mass, sometimes after Holy Communion, or after the homily, when it is deemed appropriate locally.

It's important that the ministry of readers is accorded the same respect as all the others who minister at Mass. These ministers who share God's word with God's people must be chosen carefully, given appropriate formation and commissioned publicly in the parish. Ongoing formation helps readers understand the Word they are proclaiming, so that they can read all the more effectively.

Readers have a challenging ministry. There is quite a difference between simply reading a text and proclaiming it. Ministers of the Word become more effective when they spend time beforehand becoming familiar with their text in their own Bible. This helps them decide where to pause and where to put emphasis, as well as helping them understand the context of the particular reading. Even if a reader is only responsible for one reading, all the readings for the Mass would be part of the preparation. Often, the Gospel finds an echo in the first reading and may illuminate what deserves most emphasis there.

Readings are heard as well as being proclaimed. It can help parishioners if they are also given the opportunity to prepare the readings to which they are to listen at Sunday Mass. The parish newsletter could contain the scripture references for the following Sunday to facilitate this, or copies of the following Sunday's missalette could be made available in the church.

The purchase of a Sunday missal could be recommended to parishioners, and indeed copies of reasonably priced missals could be made available by the parish at the start of the new year. The presence of a *Lectio Divina* or scripture sharing group in the parish may also help parishioners to deepen their broader knowledge of the word of God.

Communication without words: make people welcome

Every church has, at least occasionally, strangers who turn up on a Sunday morning to join in the Mass. These strangers are fellow pilgrims on the road of life; they will understand what the community really believes about God from the welcome they experience (or lack of it). According to Julian of Norwich, homeliness and courtesy are fundamental characteristics of God, seen best of all in the God who was made flesh in Jesus. It would be surprising, therefore, if these characteristics were not evident in the Christian community, especially in its welcoming of newcomers and strangers.[4]

Not all strangers are newcomers, of course. Sometimes people who have lapsed from the practice of their faith turn up for Sunday Mass, perhaps marking a significant anniversary in their own lives or at the time of bereavement. This gives a parish a rare opportunity to draw these Catholics back to full participation in the life of the Church. Some of the people who come to church on a Sunday are in a fragile state, mentally, spiritually and physically. This may be especially true of those who have drifted, but it is also true of those who are experiencing significant losses or challenges in their lives, A warm welcome can make all the difference, can make those crossing the threshold truly feel at home.[5]

The welcome at the door of the church is vital. This is partly the role of the presiding celebrant, partly the role of the community. Parishes that strongly set out to provide a welcome will see that the priest is in the churchyard before Mass, shaking hands with those coming to Mass or greeting them with love. Such parishes will also see that ministers of welcome are at the doors of the church, repeating the message of welcome in words and deeds. Sometimes a word from the altar before Mass is useful to make newcomers and strangers really feel at home. If the presider spots people at Mass he hasn't noticed before, he can repeat the welcome when he introduces the Mass.

Here are some other ways to help people feel at home:

- Provide decent welcome cards for newcomers, widely available and visible by the church doors.

- Display good quality literature about your church and community on your church noticeboard, and always include "who to contact" information.

- Train "welcomers" for ministry at the door (and indeed outside the door) who have the right gifts to greet people as they come into the worshipping assembly and provide them with service sheets etc.

- Make sure parking at your church is as painless as possible, by appointing stewards to monitor the church car park. In the interests of maintaining good relations with the broader local community, do what you can to ensure driveways aren't blocked or passing traffic impeded.

- Have decent and legible signage, inside and outside the church, so that visitors can easily find toilet facilities if they need them, or the crèche or crying room for their children (and baby-changing facilities), or the sacristy if they wish to speak with the priest.

- A church noticeboard outside will contain Mass times, the title of the church and a contact number for it, and will be sufficiently large to be read from the road.

- Use bell-ringing as a call to worship (a practice that Christians apparently learned from Islam, courtesy of St Francis' visit to the Sultan).

- The regular playing of the *Angelus* alerts newcomers to the presence of a Catholic church in their vicinity, and bells regularly chiming, up to the moment Mass begins, serve as useful reminders in the vicinity of the great event shortly to commence. (Churches in continental Europe have much to teach us about this use of bells.)

- Occasionally invite parishioners to a cup of tea or coffee after Mass at a convenient location; this serves to make newcomers feel welcome, while reinforcing their sense of belonging in long-time residents.

A sample welcome leaflet, left near the church doors or on the church noticeboard, for visitors might contain basic parish information and a little history, with words of welcome like these at the start:

WELCOME

to [name of church]
Catholic Church
whoever you may be...
A regular parishioner who feels truly
at home here
A member of the parish who hasn't been
here for a long while
A visitor attending a baptism, wedding,
funeral or First Communion
A visitor to the area staying with family
or friends
A fellow Christian seeking an oasis of
welcome and prayer
A fellow human being, looking for hope,
healing or consolation...
and perhaps like most of us here, looking for
acceptance, support, understanding,
compassion and community...[6]

Deaf people should feel at home

When considering how your parish communicates with newcomers and strangers, remember that hearing-impaired people will be among them. Remember too that acquired deafness can happen to any of us at any age. This form of deafness is often worsened by being accompanied by balance problems and tinnitus.

There are two main kinds of deafness: that caused by cochlea damage; this causes distortion, missing consonant sounds and reduced volume. The other kind of deafness is a mechanical loss that simply reduces volume. Deafness can arise from illness, infection, exposure to loud noise at work or play, head trauma, accident, tumour, genetic inheritance and, of course, old age. The Royal National Institute for the Deaf in Britain identifies one in seven of the population as having a hearing difficulty, which is quite a significant number in any congregation.

Whatever the cause of deafness in those who visit our churches, those in charge need to be aware of different ways these challenges can be met. Induction loops and good public address systems in churches (and in church halls and parish meeting-rooms) benefit hearing-aid/cochlear-implant users. An induction loop is a simple and efficient piece of equipment (literally just a loop of wire, with no electrical current, placed around the inside of the building). Any hearing-aid user sitting within the loop can hear very clearly.

If your church is equipped with a loop system, please note that it needs to be maintained. Occasionally include a note in the parish bulletin to remind people of the existence of a loop system; the note can refer people to the stewards or welcomers if they have any difficulty operating it. (It is important, therefore, to ensure that the stewards or welcomers know how to answer questions about the hearing loop helpfully and sensitively.)

Church liturgy teams should ensure that the celebrant uses a microphone when communal prayers are prayed (the Gloria, Creed, Our Father, etc.); otherwise, an eerie silence reigns for hearing-aid/cochlear-implant users. Likewise, if cantors and choirs do not have a microphone input, then the hearing-aid user is excluded from the beauty of any songs or music during the liturgy.

Some hearing-impaired people lip-read. This brings particular challenges to the parishes that try to meet their needs. Lip-readers can be facilitated by illuminating speakers' faces – especially at the lectern and celebrant's chair. This can improve perception of what is spoken or sung. Encouraging readers to slow down can also be a help. Printed liturgy sheets help hearing-impaired people to follow what is happening. "Deaf-awareness" sessions can also be arranged in the parish – especially for anyone on the pastoral team, receptionists, readers and welcomers. These sessions teach people to make eye contact when greeting people, so that deaf people can read their lips.

Sign language is used by some hearing-impaired people. When sign language is employed as part of the liturgy, encourage the signer and/or sign language interpreter to stand alongside the cantor or reader and the principal celebrant. The signer's hands are the equivalent of the celebrant's voice.[7]

SB — PAINTING A PICTURE

Luke paints a lovely picture of Peter following Jesus "from afar", and sitting in the group round the fire; then when Peter concludes his threefold denial, in a deft touch, Luke observes that "the Lord turned and looked at Peter". Then there is a daytime trial before the Sanhedrin, which is technically what the Law demands, and this is followed by the accusation before Pilate, of "turning our people upside down and stopping them paying taxes to Caesar", two lethal accusations to bring to a Roman governor. Pilate is uncomfortable, and a reference to Galilee suggests a way out, so he sends Jesus to Herod, who wants a miracle or two and doesn't get it; but Pilate and Herod become friends from that day (which is itself a miracle of sorts).

FORGIVENESS

Listen now to what Luke has Jesus say as the drama runs its course. Typical of this third Gospel, there are the women, to whom Jesus says, "Daughters of Jerusalem, don't weep over me"; then, as he is crucified, we hear him say, "Father, forgive them." His next words offer an extraordinary picture. We are not in the least surprised when one of Jesus' fellow victims insults him; but we can hardly believe our ears when the other one rebukes him and says, "Jesus – remember me when you come into your kingdom." More startling yet is Jesus' magisterial response: "Amen I'm telling you – today you are going to be with me in Paradise." We listen in awe and gaze on this picture, as Jesus' life is breathed out with the dying words, "Father, into your hands I commend my spirit." What is the mood that Luke's story arouses in you?

Mass text

ENTRANCE ANTIPHON
Rejoice, Jerusalem, and all who love her.
Be joyful, all who were in mourning;
exult and be satisfied at her consoling breast.

FIRST READING Joshua 5:9-12

PSALM Psalm 33

RESPONSE Taste and see that the Lord is good.

1. I will bless the Lord at all ti...
   his praise always on my lip...
   in the Lord my soul shall m...
   The humble shall hear and...

2. Glorify the Lord with me.
   Together let us praise hi...
   I sought the Lord and h...
   from all my terrors he s...

3. Look towards him and...
   let your faces not be ...
   This poor man called...
   and rescued him fro...

SECOND READING 2 Corinthians 5:17-21

GOSPEL ACCLAMATION
Praise and honour to you, Lord Jesus!
I will leave this place and go to my father and say:
"Father, I have sinned against heaven and against you."
Praise and honour to you, Lord Jesus!

GOSPEL Luke 15:1-3, 11-32

...ANTIPHON
...son, ...and has come to life;

@redemptorist
rp@rpbooks.co.uk

redemptorist publications

SUNDAY BULLETIN

LUKE: THE SUBLIME ARTIST

The passion narratives

This year on Palm Sunday it is Luke's version of the passion that we shall hear; today I should just like to point to some differences from what you read in Mark.

When he introduces Judas, Luke gives him a sort of excuse: "Satan had entered into Judas" (John does something of the same at 13:27 of his Gospel). For Luke, Peter and John are the two disciples who are briefed ...d to organise the Last Supper; ...d the word Luke uses for ... is the same as he ...pter 2, for the ...s no

Fr Nicholas King SJ looks at the distinctive features of Luke's passion story.

quarrel...
leader...
which...
That...
wa...
s...

ICHTHUS

ΙΧΘΥΣ

SUNDAY 12 JUNE 2
11TH SUNDAY IN ORDINARY TI...
Year

HOLY YEAR of MERCY

Choose a picture or statue to look at in church and think about it.

ENTRANCE ANTIPHON
O Lord, hear my voice, for I have called to you; be my help.
Do not abandon or forsake me. O God...

We say these words or sing a hymn as the priest approaches the altar.

We ask for God's help. Listen now to the priest as he offers this prayer.

THINK
Our readings today are all about forgiveness. Listen to how the people who have done wrong realise what they have done and are sorry. Having faith means that even if you do bad things, God will forgive you. We can all have a new start and Jesus will help us to live a good life.

LOOK at the reader and LISTEN. King David, a great soldier, poet, musician and King of Israel, turns his back on God.

The psalmist or cantor sings or says the psalm. Listen to the verses and then respond by using these words.

LOOK at the reader and LISTEN. St Paul tells his readers that nothing is more important than life with Jesus.

DO YOU KNOW?
"Reconciliation" means to bring together and be friends again. The sacrament of reconciliation is a sign and celebration which brings God's loving forgiveness to us today.

Give a shout of ...se to God, using ...words taken ...the Bible.

3rd Sunday of Easter • Divine Office Week III • Year C

SUNDAY PLUS

10 April 2016

Living the Holy Year of Mercy

Do you love me?

Tough love

by Br. Martin Horwath

What have St Peter, you and I in common? Jesus asks each of us the same question: "Do you love me?" This question prompts us to sincerely examine our response anew each day: Do I really love him? Do I get my priorities in life right: God first, neighbour second and myself last?

The prophet Jeremiah gives us an image of God as the potter. God who loved us into life made us for love, fashioning us into a suitable vessel to fulfil his purpose: to be filled with the utter fullness of God; to share with others the love we have received.

Despite God's numerous attempts to make things clearer to the people

he loves, in the form of many signs and wonders, culminating by sending his only Son as a spotless lamb sacrificed for us, human beings frequently obstruct God's plan for their true peace and happiness. As a potter, I know that clay is easier to work with than the human heart, but the Divine Potter potter refashions us, as clay that has to be moulded afresh.

This action of God can at times be tough and painful, as Peter certainly experienced in his relationship with Jesus, but God is pure love, and pure love is endlessly patient and kind. God will never give up on us. If we allow it, he will gradually mould us into a true image of his Son. Then we will be able to love him and love others as he loves us.

Br. Martin Horwath is a Cistercian monk of Mount St Bernard Abbey in Leicestershire.

Nurturing our future

by Martin O'Brien

"What's the best gift you have ever received? Who gave it to you? And why is it so special?"

This was the question asked by actors from the Ten Ten Theatre following a performance of a play called *The Gift* to a group of seven-to-nine-year-olds in a primary school.

At this particular school, a little boy put his hand up and gave the answer, "My Mum is the best gift I have ever received."

"Who gave her to you?" the actor asked.

"God," replied the boy.

"And why is she so special?"

"Because I am adopted," he said, "and without her I wouldn't be me."

The actor was very moved by this beautiful observation for there was

no doubt in this little boy's mind that he was loved unconditionally. The great sacrifices made by his adoptive parents modelled to him, in the most tangible way, the sacrificial love of Christ. What a great gift indeed!

Isn't it extraordinary how teaching children to love and be loved changes the future of their world?

Martin O'Brien is a playwright and the Artistic Director of Ten Ten Theatre.

> We forget about trust in the Lord: this is the key to success in life. Trust in the Lord! And this is a risk we must take: to trust in him, and he never disappoints.

Food for the body

by Barbara Mary Hopper

Our local food bank is staffed by volunteers from several Christian communities. Before each session we pray together, asking the Holy Spirit to guide our words and actions. People who come to us seeking food for themselves and their families are generally hesitant and feel ashamed. Over a drink and biscuits, they usually begin to relax as we listen and respond with empathy, reassurance, encouragement and sometimes with practical advice.

Before leaving with the bags of food and toiletries, they not only express their gratitude for the donors whose gifts will help them ...

realise how their deeper hunger for acceptance and respect is being satisfied when we try to respond to their needs with the mind and heart of Jesus, who asked his disciples to feed his sheep with his love.

Barbara Mary Hopper is a Catholic writer, liturgist and speaker.

Lord of my life and my love, when I am feeling alone and scared, listen to my prayers and fill me with confidence. Today, may I do some little act of kindness which might help som...

The parish newsletter is a vital communications tool [8]

The spoken word is supplemented by the written word in the parish's communication strategy. When examining the parish's communication tools, it's hard to beat the news-sheet or bulletin printed locally as a means of communication. It is underused at everyone's loss. For not only can the newsletter reinforce the words and teachings from the Sunday liturgy, it can build community in the parish and draw people together in a way that only a local production can.

What should be contained in the parish newsletter? In the first place, the newsletter contains a message relevant to the Sunday, preferably one related to the readings used at Mass, or to the liturgial season. The Sunday message may be challenging, but it should always contain an encouraging word, or at least some Good News to carry through the week.

A priest who has the facility to write can easily prepare this, or it can be delegated to another gifted parishioner, or a roster of these. Perhaps in a group of parishes, this role could be shared by suitably gifted people. If the editor is really stuck (and this can happen for various reasons in the most organised of parishes), a suitable reflection can usually be found in another publication or on some reputable Church website. No newsletter should be without this main focus, just as no Sunday Mass should be left without a homily.

Apart from its main message, each parish newsletter contains news and notices from the parish: baptisms, marriage and deaths, as soon as possible after they occur. As far as possible these notices should be personal and loving, never merely functional or without a kind wish for all involved: a prayer, a blessing, an expressive gesture on behalf of the community.

All sacramental events which occur in the parish would be reported in the local publication, but events that occur elsewhere might also be featured from time to time. Locals who may bring their child to a place that is important to them for its baptism would be congratulated also, even if this is outside the parish where they reside, as would parishioners marrying elsewhere (but only those marrying in church, obviously). People whose deaths occured in other parts of the country might also be included when their passing would leave parishioners bereft. Anything that impacts on the life of a parishioner has a place in the parish newsletter, so in addition to key sacramental moments including First Communion and confirmation of members of the parish (whether they are in school locally or elsewhere), anciliary events are also reported in it: milestone birthdays, significant wedding anniversaries, engagements, accomplishments. All parishioners' lives, their joys and sorrows, find a place in their parish's publication.

In addition to these vital features, parish newsletters are extremely useful for all kinds of parish information. Not only can the meetings of local bodies be announced, but there will usually be some space to explain these bodies, their roles and functions – and whether and how parishioners can be involved in them.[9]

The key to an effective newsletter lies in its producers. Ideally, a team of people should be involved, with each contributing according to his or her talent. Having a team involved means that too great a burden will not fall on any one volunteer. It also means that each person has a substitute to call on when unavailable to help. The newlsetter team should meet at least occasionally, and should also take breaks: many parishes suspend publication during school holidays, thus making for a newsletter which is missed and thus appreciated more – and a rested team.

A parish magazine is another option for parish communication

The process of organising a parish magazine is similar to the production of a parish newsletter, though it allows for a more relaxed deadline, being published monthly or a few times a year. As with a newsletter, a team of parishioners produces a magazine, often with their priest as part of the team. Before producing its first publication, the production team needs to agree on a "mission statement". This would clearly state what the magazine is for, whether it is to be a church production in which church-related articles will always get priority or whether it is to involve the whole local community equally, with all its various churches and organisations. What the magazine hopes to accomplish would also be included in this "mission statement", which would be published in the magazine each time.

Before launching a parish magazine, it is also important to consider the costs involved. While a parish might normally cover the cost of producing the weekly newsletter, seeing it as fundamental to its mission, this largesse might not extend to a magazine. Local advertisers might of course help, and the voluntary nature of the production team would certainly keep costs down. A cost price would be set, based on an estimate of sales and production costs. The cost should also take in the possibility of building a small surplus to fund emergencies, or of producing a bumper edition for special occasions. One option would be to set a price that might also produce a profit for a local charity (or for parish funds).

One definite advantage a parish magazine would have over a newsletter or bulletin would be space. It would certainly give parishes the possibility of including more depth in articles, more details to ponder. Photos could also be included – of parish events, of parishioners being featured for particular reasons. Articles on local history could be included too; perhaps a roving reporter might also interview locals and build up a collection of memoirs.

Your parish needs a presence on the internet

Whether or not your parish has a newsletter or parish magazine, a parish website is almost essential today, if the parish is to reach out to people on the margins, who may not be in regular contact with the church. Some use websites to find Mass times or other basic parish information; but when an attractive website is encountered, it can be a tool for greater communication and evangelisation.

It's not unknown for some people who move into an area to do a website search when they look for their new parish. The website contains clues as to the vitality of the parish and the local community. People who have lost contact with the Church use websites too, as this online forum can be a gentle, non-threatening way of getting in touch with a faith long lost, a way of testing the waters of a parish.

Getting started involves recruiting a team, people with a knowledge and interest in websites. Eager teenagers can be brought on board, as can technicians and designers who will develop and maintain the site – but the project-team need to work closely with parish leadership. A flashy local firm might get a website in shape for your parish, but they might lack basic knowledge about the Church, information which could only emanate from parish leadership or people close to the parish team. [10]

More than anything, your website needs to convey what is wonderful about your parish. If it's full of fussy notices, it gives a message that the parish is a busy place – but not necessarily a place where there is a warm welcome for everyone, where people pray and find God. Many strangers consult a website to find out the time of Mass, but having found that information, an attractive website may tempt them to align themselves more closely with the parish.

Websites also have to be right up to date. There is no point in advertising an elaborate Holy Week service when Easter has passed, just as Advent homilies look passé once Christmas arrives. This fact has to be taken into account before launching a website: a website is pointless if it doesn't change often, certainly weekly, preferably daily. Encourage your priest to post his homily after he has given it, and make sure to include the weekly newsletter in a format that allows people to download it or read it online. Emigrants in particular appreciate this link with home.

Parishioners appreciate websites that give them all sorts of parish information. Ministry rosters can be displayed so that people can check when they are next to read at Mass or when they are to act as extraordinary ministers of Holy Communion. A website also allows a parish extra space to describe in full what is involved in a baptism in the parish, or a marriage or funeral.

In rural areas, where the congregation is spread out, a well-designed website might help with parish consultations – with users contributing to parish debates and able to read the fruits of these discussions. When parishioners live a distance from a church, a visit to the parish office might not be convenient; sometimes an email address to contact can seem like an answer to prayer. [11]

Before launch, consider whether a stand-alone website best suits your needs, or whether a Facebook page might be as useful, or a page on your diocesan website. Include photos on the website as often as possible, but be sure to apply the child safeguarding rules that apply in your diocese, remembering that images of children should not be published online without the appropriate permissions of their parents or guardians.

More advanced websites include podcasts which can be streamed through the internet or downloaded onto a device. YouTube videos can also feature on your website, sourced from central Church resources.

Parish communications cannot be confined to newsletters, magazine and websites, however. Some parishes invest in technology that allows them to broadcast their masses in the local area (and even globally using the world wide web) – a godsend to elderly and housebound people. Often these have to invest in the appropriate equipment though, but sometimes the parish will assist them, either by direct grants or through fundraising or by getting local sponsorship.

No parish has all the means of communication at its unique disposal, so at least sometimes, it has to seek the help of other communicators. For a high-profile liturgy or to further spread the news about Easter and Christmas events in the church, local radio stations might be asked to carry a notice, or ads in local papers might be considered. No doubt in the future, some churches or parishes will develop apps for use with smartphones or similar services: a communications group in the parish, possibly aligned to the parish pastoral council, will ensure that parish communications continue to evolve. In a rapidly changing age of communication, no parish can afford to be left behind in employing every media to spread the Good News.

Communication is not all one-way

On these pages, many means of sharing the message of the Church and the parish have been suggested. But communication is not a one-way process; communication implies listening also, and not just in those to whom the message is directed. We, the parish practitioners, have to listen also, not only to see how well the message is being heard, but because those who listen have a role to play in communicating the Good News too, for the Holy Spirit speaks through them.

In the section on parish websites, there was a suggestion that a well-designed website could help people in large rural parishes to contribute to parish debates online and read there the fruit of those discussions. This model could be replicated in any parish, with parishioners' views and insights sought on the many challenges every parish faces: rationalisation of Mass schedules in the face of declining clergy numbers, decisions on the degrees to which churches should be maintained when the money required is not available; involvement of parishioners in parish ministries, evolving parish policies on baptisms, marriages and funerals, etc.

Sometimes, when a parish decision is needed on one of the topics suggested above, a more direct consultation exercise may be needed. As well as using the website then, pamphlets will be distributed at masses and responses sought, perhaps through a tear-out section which can be returned to a box prominently displayed in the church. Taking advice from as many as possible and coming to a decision that suits as many as possible are keys to continuing parish peace and happiness.

POINTS TO REMEMBER

☑ Jesus sent out his disciples to spread the Good News by what they said and what they did. Communication is thus at the heart of the Church's mission.

☑ Homilies, newsletters, magazines, websites and local media can help with this mission.

☑ To be effective at communication, the parish has to be flexible enough to try new ways of communicating as they become available. This may mean leaving behind media that prove ineffective.

POINTS FOR PERSONAL REFLECTION OR GROUP DISCUSSION

 What media do you use every day? Has the Christian message a presence in any of them?

What media does your parish use? Are other means of communication being neglected?

Do parishioners feel they are listened to when parish decisions are made? How can consultation be improved?

Reflection

In a higher world it is otherwise
But here below to live is to change
And to be perfect is to have changed often.

From *An Essay on the Development of Christian Doctrine*
Blessed John Henry Newman

ENDNOTES

1 From a Parish Practice article by Bernard Cotter, "The same hymn sheet", *The Tablet*, 18 August 2007.

2 Ideas on homilies from a Parish Practice article by Joseph O'Hanlon, "A word on the Word", *The Tablet*, 18 July 2009.

3 From a Parish Practice article by Bernard Cotter, "Homily truths", *The Tablet*, 29 March 2008.

4 Ideas from a Parish Practice article by Nicholas Henshall, "Divine courtesy", *The Tablet*, 4 August 2012.

5 Ideas from a Parish Practice article by Tom Grufferty, "Hospitality makes all the difference", *The Tablet*, 4 April 2005.

6 Welcome leaflet distributed at Our Lady of the Assumption Catholic Church in the Diocese of Hallam, England.

7 This section on welcoming the deaf draws on ideas from a Parish Practice article of Hilary Lagden, "Sound Advice", *The Tablet*, 30 May 2015, and from a Parish Practice article by Paul Fletcher, "A Word in your eye", *The Tablet*, 13 May 2006.

8 From a Parish Practice article by Bernard Cotter, "Well read and well informed", *The Tablet*, 15 June 2013.

9 This section on producing a parish magazine draws ideas from a Parish Practice article by Margaret Caton, "Read all about it", *The Tablet*, 26 June 2010.

10 Based on Parish website ideas from a Parish Practice article by Nicholas Henshall, "Reaching out worldwide", *The Tablet*, 13 August 2011.

11 Based on a Parish Practice article by Kate Plowman, "Worldwide web of faith", *The Tablet*, 8 September 2007.

CHAPTER 9

MAINTENANCE: *Don't let the church fall down!*

Standing outside the church building after Mass, the celebrant spots two visitors on their way out. They compliment his presiding style and looking up at the magnificent edifice towering over them, add: "You have a lovely church, Father." The priest looks at the familiar faces of his parishioners streaming past and replies: "Indeed I have – and the building's nice too."

Living stones make up the Church of God and these living stones gather in a church of bricks and mortar. Both the living stones and the bricks and mortar need maintenance, as does the pastor who is charged with minding both. This means that anyone who wants to survive working in a Catholic parish has to know something about parish maintenance.

Parishes need financial guidance

Financial maintenance is key. This is why every parish must have a finance committee; it is the essential body that ensures the church remains healthy. While the Code of Canon Law makes every other parish body in some sense conditional on diocesan norms and practices, there is no ambiguity there about the necessity of a body to regulate finance: "In each parish there is to be a finance committee to help the parish priest in the administration of the goods of the parish" (Canon 537).

It's a wise directive. No pastor could possibly have the wisdom or know-how required to supervise all the financial affairs of a parish. In the absence of a body whose advice he must seek, a priest could make unwise decisions with disastrous consequences or could be gullibly influenced by people who might not have the best interests of the parish at heart.

In most dioceses, guidelines are provided by the local bishop about the make-up of the finance committee, its term of office, membership, etc., but it usually falls to the parish priest to pick suitable members for it. The people he should choose would all be committed to faith and parish, and interested in parish development. Some might have particular skills and talents related to the tasks of a finance committee (e.g. accountants, people working in banks, public relations, etc.). People with an in-depth knowledge of the parish and its people would have a role to play also, as would those well-endowed with a broad experience of life – and common sense. In all cases, discretion would be required for members, since confidentiality would be essential for a group of people given full access to the parish's financial details.

The parish finance committee must have a certain breadth of vision in its approach to the parish. For while structures and buildings must be maintained

and projects funded, the finance committee has to keep people in mind also. Funding has to be made available to ensure the parish has the paid workers it needs, and these have to be trained appropriately and employed fairly. The finance committee has to work with an awareness of the future development of the parish also, when ordained ministers may be in shorter supply and other arrangements have to be made to ensure continuity of service in the parish (which may involve additional costs).

What to do about the buildings

The parish finance committee advises the parish priest on how to mind the parish's money, but may not be directly involved in spending it. Every parish has at least one building to maintain (the church); most have a presbytery or rectory as well, and some parishes have many more than that: chapels of ease, schools, parish halls, cemeteries, school buildings no longer in use and many more structures in varying degrees of repair.

It can be useful for a parish to have a separate committee in charge of maintaining its buildings, one responsible for all the plant, or one for each element of it. To encourage involvement, it might be advisable to

ask parishioners to elect people onto these committees, though the parish priest might also add suitable members, in consultation with the finance committee.

It's essential in arranging such committees to clarify their relationship with the finance committee from the start: the finance committee has overall responsibility for the financial affairs of the parish in its advice to the priest, while committees charged with maintaining buildings must have their expenditure cleared before any work on these structures is undertaken. In some cases, a budget can be assigned to each building committee, or else a representative from the committee charged with minding a specific building might come to the finance committee meeting with costed proposals.

If a significant building project is undertaken by the parish, it is wise to form a sub-committee to coordinate and supervise the work, implementing the funding guidelines established by the finance committee. People with relevant competencies should be involved in such groupings, along with representatives of the parish finance committee and of the parish at large.

Funds must be raised

Any parish with a debt has to keep on top of its finances so that regular repayments can be made. There is wisdom in assigning the raising of money to a specific group too. Fundraising is not everyone's "cup of tea", but some seem to take to it with aplomb. Imaginative people will often come up with interesting schemes for raising funds, with elements that may also contribute to community building (e.g. social events, neighbourhood gatherings, etc.). Sometimes grants can be got from heritage bodies or other state bodies, with appropriate canvassing: having a group solely dedicated to fundraising will mean its members can devote their energy solely to this task.

Even where parishes do not have a debt at present, the possibility of going into debt in the future can be avoided by building up funds now. Sometimes people can be more generous in contributing towards a definite project, so it is important that the fundraising committee always takes care to explain what the funds being raised will be spent on. As with building committees or groups dedicated to maintaining particular structures, the parish fundraising body would be seen as a sub-committee operating under the auspices of the finance committee and reporting regularly to it.

Is the parish priest a pastor or a manager?

The question of whether a priest is ultimately a pastor or a manager is best answered by an example from the United States. A priest in a parish there considers himself to be a very busy pastor. In an average week, he attends several meetings: Parish Finance Council, Capital Campaign, Stewardship Committee, etc. His Mondays are taken up with counting the Sunday collection, along with members of his parish team. Large segments of the year see him negotiating and renegotiating teacher contracts in the parish school, preparing the annual budget and compiling financial reports. Questioned about the pastoral activities of the parish, his stock answer would be that the laypeople run several valuable pastoral programmes very effectively.

A perfect inversion seems to be at work. The pastor spends his time involved in the kinds of commercial activities for which laypeople are trained, while the laypeople organise the pastoral work for which the pastor was trained.

This overview may be a little simplistic, but it contains a grain of truth. The pastor is not an irresponsible man, but one who takes his responsibility for the temporal goods of the parish very seriously. When he was given his current role, it was made very clear to him that where the wealth of the parish was concerned, he was to carry the ultimate responsibility. And in an American parish with up to 30 employees and annual collections amounting to hundreds of thousands of dollars, the amount of money for which he is responsible can be very considerable indeed.

In devoting such time to these matters, however, perhaps this priest is succumbing to a temptation to which priests easily fall prey – to concentrate on concrete matters and defer the rest. Work in the financial and managerial aspects of parish life can be attractive to priests because the work is satisfying, and one can see instant results. Budgets can be agreed and published, books can be balanced and agreements with employees can be settled. This stands in marked contrast with the work of pastoral planting where the results are not seen for years, if ever. A priest may well be tempted to forego the difficult work of pastoral visitation and to delegate laypeople to bring Communion to the sick and provide comfort for the dying, in his stead. They may and will carry out this work admirably, but in delegating this work entirely, the parish priest is in some sense neglecting those who are in his care.[1]

While canonically the parish priest is assigned the ultimate responsibility for the goods of the parish and must be a part of the parish finance committee, there is no need for him to be a member of any of the other bodies that report to it. Attending at the finance committee, he should hear adequate reports of the plans of all the other sub-committees and should be happy to delegate to each committee the work that it undertakes, subject to the approval of the finance committee and his agreement. This will set him free to be the carer for his flock, the role for which he was ordained.

Stewardship is worth promoting

Some parishes find that an engagement with the idea of stewardship helps to encourage parishioners to assume co-responsibility for the parish's mission. This is based on an idea imported from the US; stewardship was highlighted there in 1992 by the US Bishops' Conference as a way of responding to Pope John Paul II's challenge to the Church to engage in a "New Evangelisation".

Writing about his experience of parishes in the Merton deanery in south London, John Mulligan suggests the idea of stewardship as worthy of consideration in these islands. He explains that Christians believe they are stewards of God's resources, that everything we have belongs to God. For stewardship to work, clergy and laity must be willing and able to share trust, responsibility, ownership, development and accountability.

Stewardship is a way of living out our discipleship in the parish community and in the world. It creates an atmosphere for enabling and empowering the People of God, both lay and ordained, to share responsibility for mission, thus making a transition from maintenance to mission.

Introducing the concept of stewardship has financial implications also. Many parishes operate on a shoestring budget and struggle to provide adequate facilities for their communities to grow. Promoting the concept of stewardship means a parish depends on every member of the community taking some responsibility for development.

Many people in parishes are totally unaware of the specific financial details that shape and dictate our current status. If transparency is part of the parish package, the absolute necessity of planned giving and fundraising is perceived and understood in a shared context. When consumerism is replaced by ownership, and people know that the parish belongs to them and they belong to it, a very different model of parish is born.

Awareness and education is a vital first step to transformation. The concept of stewardship takes time, patience and effort to introduce and consolidate. Stewardship is a challenge to engage in a fairly extensive overhaul of the parochial system that has dictated and shaped parish practice for generations.[2] You will find more information on stewardship on the US Catholic Bishops' website (www.usccb.org).

Lay parish members can be often reminded that stewardship involves many ways of contributing to the parish's mission. Three Ts have been suggested as ways to make their contribution definite and concrete: Time, Treasure and Talent. Some parishioners will have the time but possibly not the financial resources to support the parish's mission, or they may have wonderful talents to make available. Their willingness to be involved will be equally accepted as those with money to share, who may not have the time to advance the projects in any other way. Stewardship works best when all are involved, according to their gifts and abilities.

The church needs attention, too

Buildings must be maintained, but the flock that gathers in them must be attended to also. The health of parishioners is as important as the health of their buildings. For this reason, a parish healthcare committee could be a useful asset for a parish, perhaps aligned to the parish finance committee. Its aim would be to keep the health of the parish and its ministers under review, for the benefit of all.

Such a committee thus could have much to do. One of the first considerations might be a parish-appointed medic for each church, someone who might be on call at times of religious services. This person might attend masses and keep an eye out for people in need of attention, whether in the pews or at the altar. This person, possibly a parish nurse, might also take a proactive role, encouraging personal health care in those in ministry, supervising rest and recreation, even checking that the priest takes time off regularly, for health and sanity.

A parish healthcare committee might also check that everything about the church building encourages health and hygiene, with clean toilet facilities available, handwashing encouraged and with special attention given to the people who touch food, particularly the Bread of Life. Sacristans, who prepare hosts before Mass and ministers who distribute them need to be reminded of the importance of clean hands. A first-aid kit in the sacristy would also be essential, another item for the health committee or professional to insist upon. Toilet facilities for handicapped people should also be provided, with care taken that the church and altar area is easily and safely accessible for people with limited mobility.[3]

What of people with special needs, like coeliacs?

One group of parishioners needing special care in a Catholic parish are coeliacs, since they cannot tolerate gluten, a constituent part of Holy Communion given under the form of bread. Coeliac disease is a common digestive condition in which the intestine has an abnormal reaction to gluten in the diet. Even a grain of gluten can cause diarrhoea and other symptoms that can last for several days. People with coeliac disease have to follow a strict gluten-free diet.

Coeliac disease affects all ethnic groups and is common in Europe and North America, as well as in southern Asia, the Middle East, North Africa and South America. Coeliac disease is, however, more common in Irish people and those of Irish descent, affecting as many as one in a hundred Irish people. This means that in parishes containing Irish people, there would be a significant number of coeliacs. No parish can presume it has no coeliacs, however – so no parish can ignore the making of pastoral arrangements for its coeliac population.

In continuity with Jewish tradition, the bread used in the celebration of the Eucharist contains unleavened wheat. Gluten-free hosts are thus ruled out, though "low-gluten" hosts are allowed; these may, however, be dangerous for some coeliacs. The CDF (Congregation for the Doctrine of the Faith) has stated that "a layperson affected by coeliac disease, who is not able to receive Communion under the species of bread, including low-gluten hosts, may receive Communion under the species of wine only" (Circular Letter to all Presidents of the Episcopal Conferences, 24 July 2003, B.1).

The simple solution, therefore, is to encourage coeliacs to receive Holy Communion from the chalice, since Catholics believe that the Body and Blood of the Lord are wholly consumed under either species. Churches must be careful to provide a chalice for coeliacs which bread has not come in contact with. Coeliacs in a parish will advise on the practical steps necessary to make Holy Communion safe for coeliacs.[4]

Who cares about the pastor?

A fictional priest who works on his own in a parish finds himself quite ill on a Saturday. The heavy cold that has weighed him down all week has turned to flu. His energy levels are low, yet he faces four weekend masses.

Out of a sense of dedication and commitment, he perseveres: he's not sure what else he can do. Things don't improve; by the last Mass, he can hardly stand. On Monday morning, he is found dead in his home. Cause of death: pneumonia.

Whose fault is his death? The priest's own, perhaps. Should he have minded himself better, got medical assistance in time, called in sick? Is it the fault of his diocese? Should better procedures have been in place, so that a priest would know what to do when ill, who to contact etc.? Or is it the fault of parishioners, who did not insist that their obviously ill priest should retire to bed and leave them without Mass? Or is it the fault of his Church, whose regulations left him without a partner to care for and support him, "in sickness and in health"?

As the fictional scenario above makes clear, the parish healthcare committee needs to have plans in place for the illness of the parish priest also. It must be clear who he contacts when ill, and who puts contingency plans into place. With enough notice, it may be possible to find a priest who will take at least some of the ill pastor's weekend masses or other urgent parish gatherings (e.g. funerals). But in cases of sudden illness, a parish must have a plan in place whereby trained lay presiders can, in an emergency, read the word of God and distribute Holy Communion to the people who have gathered expecting Mass.

Self-care is important for all who minister

For parish priests or other parish pastoral ministers to be a healthy presence in a parish, they must attend to their own care also. Christian ministers often have a difficulty that is rooted in the notion of giving oneself fully to the call to serve. The Gospel passage condemning those who put their hand to the plough and then turn from it to attend to other matters looms large for the conscientious pastoral person. The minister has to learn to balance those calls to full commitment with a vision of a Lord who called his friends also to "come away and rest awhile" (Mark 6:31). There were times when Jesus hardly had time to sleep, but there is no suggestion in the Gospel that this was a healthy state of affairs. Even for the Lord, the urgency of spreading the news of the kingdom had to be balanced with personal concerns, including the health and welfare of himself and his disciples.

Balance is the key word. There are at least three areas of life to accommodate. Firstly and most importantly, news of the Kingdom of God must be shared and the Good News of God's love told. For pastoral people, this may involve a sacramental ministry and/or a caring ministry. Put in summary form, liturgies will have to be prepared and homilies written, the sick and troubled will have to be visited, and baptisms, marriages and funerals attended to.

The second area of life the pastoral minister has to consider is his or her own family's needs. Ministers who do not have celibacy on their personal menu may have a spouse or partner whose lives they share. Even those ministers who are celibate may have parents who need time and care also, particularly as they age. Siblings and other relatives can make demands too.

The third area to hold in balance is the personal life of the minister. Maintaining personal prayer is held to be vital, but so equally is the maintenance the human and intellectual elements of the person. A pastoral minister needs time to pray every day, but also needs time to read and time to rest. The suggestion is made that each day can be divided into three time periods: morning, afternoon and evening. Two of these periods might be given over to pastoral work, but the third should be kept for the needs of the minister. To this daily oasis is added the weekly day off (twenty-four hours away from the pastoral setting) and the annual holiday, preferably taken in quarterly instalments, at the least.

A minister might find it useful to keep a record of all activities over a few weeks, to check how time is being spent. It can be eye-opening to realise how many hours each day and week are given over to work and how few to personal time. Having a supervisor may help the minister achieve a balance. A chat with a doctor or a counsellor may be useful to the same end.[5]

Moving house and parish affects every priest

Moving to a new parish must be good for a priest's humility; it certainly shatters his illusions every time it happens. After a few years in a parish, a priest attains a certain level of comfort. He begins to get to know parishioners individually; he starts to have the confidence to call them by their Christian names. Anyone in ministry will be familiar with the sense of well-being this brings. A move to another assignment shatters this and brings the minister back to the bottom again. It's not easy to move on and start again.

The years spent by a minister in any assignment can be likened to a hill being climbed. One starts at the bottom of the hill, unknown by anyone in the place where one is to minister, and innocent to the struggles the climb will bring. Slowly the mountain is climbed, and fellow climbers become familiar. Through listening, the minister learns about those who made the climb before, their pitfalls and their victories. Over months and years, the place of ministry becomes familiar, as do the others who struggle there.

Then, the minister reaches the summit, or close to it. From this vantage point, the assignment looks different; slowly, over the years, it has changed from being a foreign and strange place to a community where one feels at home, accepted, maybe even loved. And from there the minister is unceremoniously and usually abruptly parachuted to another assignment, to start at the bottom of the hill once again.

The first year in a parish is a year of listening. One must learn everything about the new place, from the mouths of those who live there. One might have a preconceived notion of what is needed, but it might be completely at variance with the truth. Time spent listening will teach. A priest might also have a preconceived notion of his predecessors. Much humility is required as he learns what kinds of people they really were.

A colleague told me the two words he had learned to say *ad nauseam* in his first year in a new parish: "Oh yes?" When people told him that his predecessor was an alcoholic and a gambler, he said, "Oh yes?" just as when others commended his holiness and preaching. Listening to the heart of people's comments, he learned the truth about the priest who preceded him, as well as the key expectations of people in the parish towards their priest. The experience also taught how little can be learned by one who cannot listen.

Moving to a new assignment is difficult on so many levels. It combines elements of the three greatest causes of depression in most people's lives: grief (at the loss of many co-workers and friends), moving house, and changing job. Depression is inevitable. Energy can be low, which, ironically, makes it easier for one to make no change.

Settling in can take anything from a year to eighteen months. Certainly, one has to go through a full year in a new place and all the times and seasons and traditions of the year there before beginning to feel at home. In time comes understanding; one learns why silly mistakes were made in the past and how to avoid making similar ones, as well as learning who the key people in the parish are – rarely the names recorded in the parish "Who's Who". One learns what makes the place unique – and what one can contribute to it. Everything is possible with patience, and humility.

The priest recently moved from a parish where he was perfectly at home and much loved will surely have plenty of the latter – and the depression and lethargy that follow a move may bring the former.[6]

The future: parish priest or parishes' priest?

More than likely, the parish priest of tomorrow will have more than one parish under his care. His personal maintenance in health and strength will be even more of a challenge then. This is the story of Fr Geert C. Leenknegt who gradually accumulated five parishes in the Diocese of Ghent, Belgium:

It all began at the end of 2000 when Arthur Luysterman, the Bishop of Ghent, appointed me to St Macharius' parish in Laarne. He told me I was likely to get a second smaller parish within a couple of years. Knowing this in advance made it easier to consider the kind of parish development I would be facing.

We became two in 2003 when I was asked to be parish priest of St Annaparish in Wetteren-ten-Ede. With the nomination of a non-resident parish priest, the community cohesion there was fragmented. It is never easy for two parishes to get used to the idea of sharing one parish priest.

And then in 2006, there were five when I was asked to be parish priest of three more parishes. Although we had six months to prepare for the change, it took more than three years to deal with the issues that arose. People were unhappy they no longer had a resident priest; the geographical distance between the five parishes did not make things easy, and, most painfully, some of the pastoral co-workers found it difficult to cope.

It took seven years before these five parishes began growing towards pastoral cooperation. Good communication, adequate consultation and ample preparation time was very important for growth in mutual solidarity between different parish communities. It was also important that parish teams, wishing to cooperate or to merge, have a mutual sensitivity to the differences in the parishes.

In our diocese, the plan was to redesign parish structures by 2020. Our parish team has already begun the preparations to become one large parish with this new structure. The priest will not be there to serve five parishes, but for one collaborative pastoral entity. To emphasise this new entity, we have reduced our celebrations of Sunday Mass from five to just two inter-parochial celebrations. The liturgical collaborators from all the parishes take turns to ensure that there is a lector, an acolyte, a cantor and other liturgical ministers.

Building one parish out of five communities is stimulated by encouraging friendships between all the parishioners. Organisation is essential and one group of people who must not get lost in the changes is the sick and the lonely. For the less mobile, a car-pooling system is very important. Recognising that we come together as the family of God in Christ is the most important aspect of this transition.[7]

POINTS TO REMEMBER

- A parish's finance committee is essential, with a sub-committee responsible for maintaining buildings.
- Try to make sure that the pastor spends his time doing the pastoral work for which he was trained; and let the laypeople spend their time with the kinds of commercial activities for which they are trained.
- Stewardship helps to encourage parishioners to assume co-responsibility for the parish's mission.
- Care is important: care for the parishioners, care for the ministers and self-care.

POINTS FOR PERSONAL REFLECTION OR GROUP DISCUSSION

- Think about what it would be like for laypeople if they had to move house every time they changed jobs – and consider what support you might give a new priest.
- Imagine building one parish out of five communities and consider how it might work in your area – taking into account Fr Geert C. Leenknegt's experience.
- What part can you play in your parish if it merges with another two or three parishes?

Prayer

Gracious and loving God, you are with us on our journey and you strengthen us as we build communities. Help us to remember those who have gone before us and built the communities of the past. Enable us to focus on being loving, serving, worshipping communities. Empower us to appreciate all that has been, embrace all that is and be faithful and help develop all that will be. We ask this in the name of Christ, our Lord and through the power of the Holy Spirit. Amen.

ENDNOTES

1 From a Parish Practice article by Bernard Cotter, "Putting first things first", *The Tablet*, 21 February 2009.

2 From a Parish Practice article by John Mulligan, "Towards stewardship", *The Tablet*, 17 May 2014.

3 From a Parish Practice article by Bernard Cotter, "Minister to the ministers", *The Tablet*, 29 January 2011.

4 Based on a Parish Practice article by Bernard Cotter, "Take this cup", *The Tablet*, 23 June 2012.

5 From a Parish Practice article by Bernard Cotter, "Burnout helps no one", *The Tablet*, 19 July 2008.

6 From a Parish Practice article by Bernard Cotter, "Entrance Strategy", *The Tablet*, 22 November 2008.

7 From a Parish Practice article by Geert C. Leenknegt, "Happily extended family", *The Tablet*, 22 June 2013.

CHAPTER 10

OUTREACH: *The Church exists for those who don't belong*

One of my teachers once said that the Church is the only organisation that exists for the benefit of those who do not belong.[1] At the time, I thought it was a strange thing to say; and I know that many people in the class agreed with me. It's not that we didn't want to help the poor and downtrodden and needy; and, it wasn't that we didn't think we should bring the Good News to others. We were thinking that we parishioners have a responsibility to support our communities and parishes financially, emotionally and spiritually – and this should mean that we parishioners should benefit from this support before all others. It seemed countercultural to think about outsiders to that extent.

Having said that, this concept of the Church being for the benefit of all its members is nothing new. In the Great Commission (Matthew 28) Jesus tells us to "Go make disciples of all nations." Jesus never stopped sharing the Good News; that's what he calls people in parishes to do, too. And anyone who wants to survive working in a Catholic parish has to understand that outreach is at the core of what we do.

Parishes reach out to people on the edge

Every parish contains people who used to be part of it, but, for some reason, no longer continue to be an active part of it. The most obvious group of these are people who cannot participate in the parish's life because of illness or a change of personal circumstances.

Sick and housebound people and those in nursing homes need to be assured that their place is not lost because they can no longer come to Mass. In an ideal world, Communion is brought to them by the priest occasionally and by lay ministers every Sunday; and, with the Bread of Life, comes the Sunday's readings sheet, the parish newsletter and every other bit of news that will interest housebound people and make them feel that they are still part of their parish.

The sick might be invited to join a prayer circle to involve them in the life of the parish: they can undertake to back a parish project with their prayers and sacrifices, while the parish in return undertakes to remember them in prayer at the Sunday Mass.

Others on the parish's edge can include people deprived of membership of a loving family by various circumstances: people living alone in poor conditions, in flats and bedsits, people recovering from addictions, the homeless and lost people – and the children of those who are unable to take care of them. Every parish worthy of the name "Christian" keeps such people in its sights and creatively tries to draw them into the arms of the parish community through occasional social events or even a "cuppa" after weekday or Sunday Mass can help integrate marginalised people and create lasting friendships.

Parishes remember those who have stopped coming to Mass

A story from a Catholic parish illustrates the value of a community keeping in contact with its members. A parishioner met someone she used to see at Mass in the supermarket and realised he had not seen him for a while. "I stopped coming to Mass over a year ago," he said. "Nobody seemed to notice or care, and the parish priest never visited me to find out why."

Traditionally, priests visited homes in their parishes, but declining members of clergy mean that this will not be possible for much longer. This is a role laypeople can take on, with formation and support. Sheila Keefe, who is involved in the "Celebrating Family" project in Portsmouth Diocese, wrote in *The Tablet* about how this might work.[2]

She writes that households to be visited in the parish are sent an introductory letter from their parish priest two weeks before the anticipated visit, with a contact address in case they choose not to be visited. In most cases, members of visitation teams are welcomed. Churchgoers are asked what they like and dislike about the parish, what changes they would like to see, what activities they would like to take part in.

An information pack given to each household includes a prayer, the parish newsletter, details of parish activities with contact details, and bookmarks for the children. Housebound parishioners are put in touch with the Society of St Vincent de Paul; some of them are offered a lift to one of the Sunday masses and others are told about internet links to masses they can find online. Singers are given details of the parish choir; the lonely are introduced to the parish lunch club; those interested in youth work, sport, justice and peace, or ecumenism are all introduced to the groups concerned.

In these visits, conversations can turn to discussions ranging from faith, prayer and the Church's teachings to the challenges of parenthood, sickness, and ageing. Sometimes, the visitors are concerned that they would not know the "answers" to questions people might raise. In practice, though, they find most people are not looking for answers, they just want to share their experiences. If they don't know the answer to a question, the visitor can simply say: "I'll find out for you and let you know."

A parish dilemma: what to do when non-practising Catholics ask for the sacraments

What happens when a non-practising Catholic comes to the parish wanting a child baptised, wanting to be married or wanting a relative to have a Catholic funeral? While no one who lives in the territory of a particular parish can be deprived of its care, committed Catholics there often wonder why they must provide their church free of charge for the baptisms, marriages and funerals of people who contribute little else to the life of the community. It is a dilemma.

They might argue that, since the parish cannot be effective without the help and ministry of at least some of its residents, it should ask that those who wish to take an active role would make their presence known. Some American parishes formalise this by penalising those who do not do so, levying an inflated charge for the parish's services for the non-registered.

Laypeople are called to "engage zealously in the Church's apostolic works; they attract people toward the Church who had been perhaps very far away from it; they ardently cooperate in the spread of the word of God, particularly by catechetical instruction; by their expert assistance they increase the efficacy of the care of souls as well as of the administration of the goods of the Church" (*Apostolicam Actuositatem*, Decree on the Apostolate of the Laity, 10).

To help both priests and people achieve these tasks, registration of members of a parish is proposed. This supports both priests and laypeople as they strive to fulfil their obligations to support the mission and needs of the parish. It is a routine step for Catholics in US parishes. It is also proposed in countries such as Ireland, where the majority of the population are Catholic but may be uninvolved in the life of their local parish.

There is a tension between looking inward and looking outward

A lot of the stress in parishes stems from the tension between looking inward and looking outward – between pastoral care with the parish and reaching out to the wider community (and the world). Everyone has an opinion on which one of these three is most important. Of course they must all be attended to simultaneously, which is difficult especially when it comes to budgeting the limited number of hours in a clergy-person's day, as well as budgeting financial resources.

Parishes are most effective when they hold these three perspectives in creative tension – not by saying "no" to one at the expense of the other but by saying "yes" to all three. This doesn't mean burning out the clergy and lay leaders in trying to be all things to all people but rather identifying those with gifts in each approach and encouraging them – while simultaneously educating the entire congregation about the fact that these demands are not mutually exclusive.

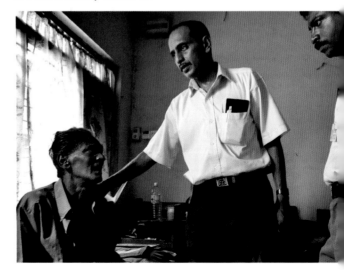

Every church can welcome the lapsed

Numerous programmes for bringing back the lapsed can easily be sourced on church websites. These "Bringing-back-the-lapsed" programmes usually have a number of elements – typically welcome, listening, input and ritual. The lapsed are identified and targeted. A "crack team" of committed parishioners are sent out with the aim of attracting them to an evening or evenings. Ads are placed and parishioners are encouraged to coax the non-Massgoers to come along.

The subsequent programme can take different forms. There will probably be a listening element, with people who have not felt part of the Church for years given the opportunity to vent their frustrations. There will probably be input also, as the committed (and perhaps even a visiting expert) are given the chance to put their own case forward, countering the doubts and frustrations. At the end of the programme, there may be a ritualised welcome, a procession into the worship space, a splash of baptismal water symbolising re-entry into the parish community. Ideally, these programmes should run continuously – or, at least, when there are one or two "returners".

The big question for these programmes is what we are bringing the lapsed back to! If it is to boring homilies, dead liturgies, children made feel unwelcome and a minimalist approach to parish life, we are in trouble. The best the Church can offer the lapsed is a lively and involving parish community where they will feel welcome, involved and at home, every Sunday.

The lapsed are not fools. They know when a parish is alive: it shows. People who attend Mass are happy to be there; everyone sings. Old and young alike are involved in the ministries. The sick are visited, nursing homes and hospitals, too. The Sunday homily is well prepared, with a cheerful presider who makes himself available to people before or after Mass. The building itself is heated, bright and clean – and microphones work. It's clear that people are involved in the life of the place, that they feel it's theirs. No one person does everything.

A weekly newsletter should be available at all masses with an occasional headline-grabbing event to capture the imagination – an ecumenical service, visiting choir or fundraising event for victims of famine or earthquake (with posters and publicity widely spread). A special welcome can be given to all children and visitors at weekend liturgies; and those too young to receive Communion (as well as anybody else who is not receiving Communion for any reason) can be invited to come forward for a blessing. Any ongoing effort to improve parish life for all is the best attraction a parish can offer.[3]

Welcome strangers to your church

In 2008, the then Archbishop, Vincent Nichols, commissioned nearly forty volunteers to operate a "Seeker's Centre" at St Michael's Parish, at the heart of the shopping district in Birmingham. Their aim was to invite in at least some of the thousands of people who walked by the church daily, perhaps just to pay a visit, but perhaps to introduce some to Christ and to Catholicism.

Many of the first volunteers had little or no experience of outreach, but they were willing to learn. To get things started, several vision and training afternoons were put on, supported by CASE, the Catholic Agency to Support Evangelisation. These sessions covered topics such as recent Church teaching on evangelisation, and some of the main methods and processes used in evangelisation. The team was also given a clear brief to develop and was encouraged to put into practice the aims of the mission, which were to provide a warm welcome and hospitality, to listen, pray, journey spiritually with visitors, share their faith stories and to create a pleasant and peaceful environment for both visitors and volunteers.

The team decided that the church would be open every weekday afternoon, staffed by volunteers from 2 until 5pm and they had a number of Spirit-filled encounters. For example, a young Polish girl who was desperately homesick came into the church. Some of the volunteers who speak Polish talked with her, offered the hands of friendship and reassured her that her homesickness would lessen in time. Another day, some of the volunteers heard someone sobbing at the front of the church. As they approached the sanctuary, they saw a young African man kneeling in front of the tabernacle in a state of distress. They sat with him as he cried. Eventually, he told the volunteers that he had been a child soldier in his home country and was made to do some terrible things. He was in a state of despair – convinced that God would never forgive him for what he had done. The volunteers listened to him and reminded him of God's unconditional love. Through the concern they showed for him, he was able to experience the forgiveness he so yearned for.[4]

Conversations with strangers are part of a church's mission

St Mary-on-the-Quay did something similar a few years ago in Bristol. At the time, they had a lunchtime Mass every weekday at 12.15pm for a congregation made up of city workers or those who come into the city centre to do some shopping, or staff and occasional visitors from the five hospitals nearby. On Friday evenings, there was also a 5.30pm Mass for a congregation of people finishing their work in the shops and offices. Vagrants seeking shelter and warmth (especially in the winter) would also come into the church from time to time – and people who were waiting for ongoing buses or trains and had a little time on their hands would take the opportunity to attend Mass.

Because the numbers of people were comparatively few (by comparison with the number of people who came for Sunday Masses), the core of the congregation was regular and a real community spirit grew out of the Massgoers. Marion Morgan wrote an article in *The Tablet* saying that what she most appreciated about these weekday Masses was the feeling of space. In some cases, people were looking for an anonymous space where they could pray or cry or rejoice without being seen or recognised. They came from all over, gravitating to this city centre parish and finding a haven.

When people have left the church at the end of Mass, there is often a chance to greet someone at the back of the church idly turning over the books and papers. Sometimes, this leads to a conversation and an invitation to join one or two others for coffee (or even something stronger). This kind of mission and ministry is one that anyone can engage in. It is a pastoral ministry that was once thought the province of the priest; but it is one that the laity can, of course, provide fruitfully. This kind of listening is something we can all practise. Nearly all of us have had experiences of listening – or being listened to – through a chance conversation on a train or bus. Or, maybe, it was an opportunity to let off steam with a stranger we would never see again – or offering a word of encouragement to someone who needed it.[5]

Caring for the homeless

More and more parishes provide emergency accommodation to street homeless and those at immediate risk of sleeping rough locally. The projects normally run between December and March each year. The projects are often run by a few churches of various denominations who all have the same heart – and who want to reach out to the homeless and provide warmth, food, security and hope. There is usually a set venue for each night of the week which is manned by twenty to thirty volunteers per night. Through the partnerships of local churches the project has a unique ability to meet the practical needs of homeless individuals without discrimination or favour.

The St Vincent de Paul Society makes 12,000 "Vinnie Packs" for homeless people and people in hostels throughout England and Wales each winter. Parishes contribute to the SVP for these Vinnie Packs, which contain a Thinsulate thermal hat, thermal socks and thermal gloves, a tube of toothpaste, toothbrush, and a foil blanket, pen and information sheet.

Caring for the hungry

Every day people in our country go hungry. Many parishes, schools, businesses and individuals in England and elsewhere donate non-perishable, in-date food to foodbanks local to them. There are a number of different models of foodbanks. In one model, frontline care professionals such as doctors and social workers identify people in crisis and issue a food voucher. Other models operate an open-user system; and we've heard of a system where a person asks a person of responsibility in the parish for a key to a well-stocked pantry, where they are allowed to take what they need.

Hunger is not just a Third World problem. Today people in our country will struggle to feed themselves and their families. Redundancy, illness, benefit delay, domestic violence, debt, family breakdown and paying for heating during winter are just some of the reasons why people go hungry. Foodbanks are always looking for volunteers, as are the St Vincent de Paul Society, who provide many of these services in Ireland.

Caring for prisoners and their families

PACT (Prison Advice and Care Trust) is a Catholic charity that supports prisoners and their families in making a fresh start and works in several prisons across London. They rely on the dedication, skills and generosity of volunteers to help those in need. Parishes adjacent to prisons in other parts of Great Britain and Ireland would do well to set up similar charities to help prisoners.

The Irish Council for Prisoners Overseas (ICPO) is a charitable organisation established by the Irish Catholic Bishops' Conference in 1985, which works on behalf of Irish prisoners in jails outside Ireland and their families. Parishes interested in this kind of outreach can make contact through the Irish Chaplaincy in London (www.irishchaplaincy.org.uk).

Migrants, refugees and asylum seekers need care, too

In our time, migration is growing on a worldwide basis. Victims of violence and poverty are forced to leave their homelands with dreams of a safer and better future. If they survive the abuses and hardships of the journey, they then have to face suspicions and fear of the people and the authorities they encounter when they get where they are going.

We hear the arguments of the politicians who claim there is no space for these people; meanwhile, they are not offering clear and practical policies regulating the acceptance of migrants and providing for short- or long-term programmes of integration which are respectful of the rights and duties of all. It seems that today, more than in the past, our consciences are troubled and we no longer take the suffering of others for granted.

We must find ways of responding which, grounded in the theological virtues of faith, hope and charity, find practical expression in works of spiritual and corporal mercy. And, we must remember that migrants are our brothers and sisters in search of a better life, far away from poverty, hunger, exploitation and the unjust distribution of the planet's resources which are meant to be equitably shared by all.[6]

If your parish doesn't do anything for migrants, refugees and asylum seekers, why not consider setting something up? The centres for migrants and refugees offer various services and advice and support, and are often in need of volunteers and extra resources. Alternatively, you could do something as simple as offering free English classes for people once a week for a few hours in your parish hall. Some volunteers work with deaf people; but you need to be able to lip-read and speak English at an intermediate level; some volunteers are simply conversation partners. These are people who commit to half an hour to an hour for each student and it simply involves speaking English so that the student can practise their language skills.

Care of the planet and climate change

Climate change is real, urgent and it must be tackled. The climate is a common good, belonging to all and meant for all. Mark Dowd points out that the "talk on the subject has been talked". Now, the question is how parishes can set about "walking the walk". In his article on Pope Francis' encyclical, *Laudate Si'*, he asks how Catholics can become beacons of hope in our environmentally degraded world.

As Catholics, we have the benefit of a solid tradition of virtue ethics. Put simply, if something is worth doing, it is valuable not only for its consequences, but because it is worth doing in itself. Small actions can be genuinely sacramental: outward signs of a rich interior disposition. We are being challenged not to think of practices such as adopting renewable energy, eating less meat and walking to Mass as "lifestyle fads" or consumer choices, but as an integrated show of our bond with God and the material world he has created.

We could stop to give thanks to God before and after meals to make us aware of the relationship of bounty and dependency between humans and the natural world. If suitable materials were provided, parishes could feature care of creation in preparation for Holy Communion and confirmation in their catechetics programmes.[7]

Ethical banking

Investment banking has suffered profoundly in the popular press and there are good reasons for the outcry. But, investment banking does contribute to the common good by matching capital with valid economic needs. When it does so with efficiency and integrity, communities flourish.

John Terrill, Director for the Center for Integrity in Business at Seattle Pacific University, wrote that when considering pay policy, companies must take into account issues of internal equity (fairness of pay across jobs within an organisation), as well as external equity (competitiveness of pay relative to comparable jobs in competitive companies and industries).

Both are important, but for Christians who have opportunities to set or influence the policy agenda, there is a third benchmark – biblical equity. To remain competitive, matters of internal and external equity

must be part of the solution, but let those conversations be influenced by creative new ideas with a solid foundation of biblical equity. Christians working in the investment banking field in positions to set or influence policy must make sure their voices are heard.[8]

Catholic social teaching

There is a body of teaching in the Catholic Church, which is sometimes called "the Church's best-kept secret" because most people have little or no knowledge of it. And yet, it often ignites real interest and passion, especially in the young.

Catholic social teaching stems from the "Great Commandment" to put God first and to love your brother and sister as yourself – acting as if what happens to them also happens to you.

> *"Teacher, which commandment in the law is the greatest?" Jesus said to him, "'You shall love the Lord your God with all your heart, and with all your soul, and with all your mind.' This is the greatest and first commandment. And a second is like it: 'You shall love your neighbour as yourself.' On these two commandments hang all the law and the prophets."*
>
> Matthew 22:36-40

The issues covered in the Church's social teaching can be broadly categorised into the following themes: human dignity; the option for the poor; the dignity of work; solidarity; Catholic teaching on poverty: a place at the table; faithful citizenship: a call to political responsibility; social justice; human and economic development; and on social sin.

In 2012, Pope Benedict XVI's New Year message addressed the need to educate young people in the urgent issues of justice and peace. He addressed all those responsible for educating and forming young people, pointing out that real education is "in truth and freedom" (*Educating Young People in Justice and Peace*, 3), the source of which is God. Young people, he said, must be educated in justice because this is at the very heart of who we are as human beings. We must see this as being in solidarity and love for all people. Peace, he said, is both a divine gift and a human task and responsibility:

In order to be true peacemakers, we must educate ourselves in compassion, solidarity, working together, fraternity, in being active within the community and concerned to raise awareness about national and international issues and the importance of seeking adequate mechanisms for the redistribution of wealth, the promotion of growth, cooperation for development and conflict resolution.

Educating Young People in Justice and Peace, 5

With his election, Pope Francis – who, as he himself said, came "from the ends of the earth" – picked up this theme. In his first week as pope, he spoke of the need for the Church to be seen as "poor and for the poor". In taking the name Francis, after St Francis of Assisi, he was paying tribute to someone who was totally dedicated to serving the poor and marginalised. It was seen by many as another indication that the Church is making it an urgent priority to respond to the cry of the poor wherever they are found.

Where did it start?

Based on God's revelation in Christ, the Church has been developing its body of social teaching as long as it has existed. Catholic social teaching first began to be formulated as a system in the late nineteenth century. Pope Leo XIII is credited with having introduced it in 1891 with his encyclical *Rerum Novarum*. Successive popes have added to and developed it, principally in the form of encyclicals (letters). These have Latin titles – but don't let that put you off. They are all translated into accessible English. The quickest way to find the texts is to go online and type in the title. The Vatican website is a very good place to start: www.vatican.va. There, you will find:

- *Rerum Novarum* (On the Condition of Labour) – Pope Leo XIII, 1891

- *Quadragesimo Anno* (After Forty Years) – Pope Pius XI, 1931

- *Mater et Magistra* (Christianity and Social Progress) – Pope John XXIII, 1961

- *Pacem in Terris* (Peace on Earth) – Pope John XXIII, 1963

- *Gaudium et Spes* (Pastoral Constitution on the Church in the Modern World) – Vatican Council II, 1965

- *Populorum Progressio* (On the Development of Peoples) – Pope Paul VI, 1967

- *Octogesima Adveniens* (A Call to Action) – Pope Paul VI, 1971

- *Justicia in Mundo* (Justice in the World) – Synod of Bishops, 1971

- *Laborem Exercens* (On Human Work) – Pope John Paul II, 1981

- *Sollicitudo Rei Socialis* (On Social Concern) – Pope John Paul II, 1987

- *Centesimus Annus* (The Hundredth Year) – Pope John Paul II, 1991

- *Evangelium Vitae* (The Gospel of Life) – Pope John Paul II, 1995

- *Fides et Ratio* (Faith and Reason) – Pope John Paul II, 1995

- *Deus Caritas Est* (God is Love) – Pope Benedict XVI, 2005

- *Sacramentum Caritatis* (Apostolic Exhortation on the Eucharist) – Pope Benedict XVI, 2007

- *Caritas in Veritate* (Charity in Truth) – Pope Benedict XVI, 2009

As these documents show, Catholic social teaching concerns just about everything that needs to be put right and transformed, to enable the beauty and dignity of all people to shine. Take a look at some of these quotations from Church documents. Pay attention to how challenging and radical they are – not what you might expect from the Church. But, they all inform what we do in a Catholic parish under the headings of spiritual, moral, social and cultural education. *The Common Good* was produced in 1996 by the Bishops' Conference of England and Wales. You can find this document and further resources by visiting and following the links at www.catholicsocialteaching.org.uk.

Here are some key quotes on Catholic social teaching from *The Common Good*:

Each generation takes the natural environment on loan, and must return it after use in as good or better condition as when it was first borrowed. (107)

State welfare provision [is not] a desirable substitute for payment of a just wage. (98)

The defeat of Communism should not mean the triumph of unbridled capitalism. (Introduction)

The nation's real crisis is not economic, but moral and spiritual. (113)

We believe that it is in the growing priority of technology over ethics, in the growing primacy of things over persons, and in the growing superiority of matter over spirit, that the most serious threats to British society now lie. (118)

Excessive economic and social inequalities within the one human family, between individuals and between peoples, give rise to scandal and are contrary to social justice, to equality, and to the dignity of the human person, as well as to peace within society and at the international level. (Appendix I, citing *Gaudium et Spes*, 29.2)

In his desire to have and to enjoy rather than to be and to grow, man consumes the resources of the earth and his own life in an excessive and disordered way. (Appendix I, citing *Centesimus Annus*, "The Hundredth Year", 37)

What are the principles of Catholic social teaching?

Humanity is one family despite differences of nationality or race.

The Bishops of England and Wales, The Common Good, 14

This is at the heart of Catholic social teaching, and means that:

- We all make up the People of God – there are no outsiders!

- We are all part of the Body of Christ – there are no dismembered bits!

- We are all called to live in communion – as one – with ourselves, each other and God.

The preferential option for the poor

People who are poor and vulnerable have a special place in Catholic social teaching: this is what is meant by the "preferential option for the poor".

The poor are not a burden; they are our brothers and sisters. Christ taught us that our neighbourhood is universal: so loving our neighbour has global dimensions… Solidarity with our neighbour is also about the promotion of equality of rights and equality of opportunities; hence we must oppose all forms of discrimination and racism.

The Bishops of England and Wales, The Common Good, 14

With this comes considerable responsibility for the choices we make – to act or not to act. We are all accountable:

The joys and hopes, the grief and anguish of the people of our time, especially those who are poor or afflicted, are the joys and hopes, the grief and anguish of the followers of Christ.

Pastoral Constitution on the Church in the Modern World, Gaudium et Spes, 1

Scripture tells us that every human being is made in the image of God, so each individual is the clearest reflection of God among us. Accordingly, the Catholic social vision has as its focal point the human person – whatever their social status, demographic, background, ethnicity, attractiveness, education:

Christ challenges us to see his presence in our neighbour, especially the neighbour who suffers or who lacks what is essential to human flourishing.

The Bishops of England and Wales, The Common Good, 17

Catholic social teaching in the daily life of the parish

The social teaching of the Church is a response to people's longings to answer the cry of the poor and marginalised, and Catholic education seeks to offer young people something worth committing to – a faith that is lived in action for justice. The key word here is "action". *The principle of Catholic social teaching is that from a "living faith" comes "loving action", which brings about transformation into a "civilisation of love".*[9] The task of priests, catechists and parish pastoral workers (in the widest possible sense of the word) is to enable and encourage those they meet in the parish to bring about change where it is needed. This can be a challenging process, involving self-sacrifice, humility and letting go of our fixed ideas about ourselves and one another – but it must be demonstrated by our actions.

Parishes should be keen to be actively engaged in action for social justice. In harnessing young people's enthusiasm, drive and energy, they usually excel in both the scope of what they undertake and the results – for example, fundraising and charitable activities. There are many charities willing and able to support the parish in promoting Catholic social teaching – their aim is to ensure that it is a lived reality rather than a taught theory. You will find some of these charities listed at the back of the book.

You must be the change you want to see in the world.

Mahatma Gandhi

 POINTS TO REMEMBER

☑ Focus on what you do well in your parish – and try to do it better!

☑ Engage an outside specialist if you are unsure about anything. The agencies mentioned in this chapter and those listed at the back of the book will give their time and expertise for free.

POINTS FOR PERSONAL REFLECTION OR GROUP DISCUSSION

Reflect on this saying: *The Church exists for the benefit of those who do not belong.*

⚡ In what ways does it resonate with you or challenge you?

⚡ How is this tension played out in your own community of faith?

⚡ Has it been creative or destructive?

What can we do to better communicate this message?

Prayer

Pax Christi daily prayer
Thank you loving God
for the gift of life
for this wonderful world which we all share
for the joy of love and friendship
for the challenge of helping to build your kingdom.

Strengthen
my determination to work for a world of peace and justice
my conviction that, whatever our nationality or race,
*   we are all global citizens, one in Christ*
my courage to challenge the powerful with the values of the Gospel
my commitment to find nonviolent ways of resolving conflict —
*   personal, local, national and international*
my efforts to forgive injuries and to love those I find it hard to love.

Teach me
to share the gifts you have given me
to speak out for the victims of injustice who have no voice
to reject the violence which runs through much of our world today.

Holy Spirit of God
renew my hope for a world free from the cruelty and evil of war,
so that we may all come to share in God's peace and justice.
Amen.

Pax Christi (UK) members' daily prayer

ENDNOTES

[1] Some would attribute this quote to William Temple, Archbishop of Canterbury (1942–1944), theologian, scholar, and advocate for social justice.

[2] From a Parish Practice article by Sheila Keefe, "Way back to the fold", *The Tablet*, 28 January 2006.

[3] From a Parish Practice article by Bernard Cotter, "Bring them back to life", *The Tablet*, 8 July 2006.

[4] From a Parish Practice article by Clare Ward, "A model for mission", *The Tablet*, 13 September 2008.

[5] From a Parish Practice article by Marion Morgan, "Off-peak savings", *The Tablet*, 23 August 2008.

[6] Inspired by Pope Francis: Message of His Holiness Pope Francis for the World Day of Migrants and Refugees 2016, (17 January 2016), (©Libreria Editrice Vaticana, from the Vatican, 12 September 2015).

[7] From a Parish Practice article by Mark Dowd, "The wheels are in motion", *The Tablet*, 3 August 2015.

[8] Excerpts from an article by John Terrill, Director for the Center for Integrity in Business at Seattle Pacific University, "A new kind of equity for Wall Street Reform", 31 March 2010 (http://blog.spu.edu/cib/2010/03/31/a-new-kind-of-equity-for-wall-street-reform), accessed 8 April 2016.

[9] Michael J. Schultheis, *Our Best Kept Secret: The Rich Heritage of Catholic Social Teaching*, (CAFOD, London, 1988), 6. See also *Compendium of the Social Doctrine of the Church* (http://www.vatican.va/roman_curia/pontifical_councils/justpeace/documents/rc_justpeace_doc_compendio-dott-soc_en.html), accessed 21 March 2013.

APPENDIX I
Addressing the clergy: an essential guide

This is a "how-to" guide for corresponding with church people in the Catholic Church. *
(Usually, the title at the start of a letter indicates how a person is to be addressed in person.)
For a "who's who" guide, see Chapter 1.

Addressing the Pope
On the envelope: "His Holiness Pope N., Apostolic Palace, 00120 Rome, Italy"
- At the beginning of a letter: "Your Holiness" or "Most Holy Father"

Addressing a cardinal
On the envelope: "His Eminence Cardinal [First Name, Surname] Cardinal Archbishop of [Location]"
- At the beginning of a letter: "Your Eminence" or "Dear Cardinal [Surname]"

Addressing an archbishop
On the envelope: "The Most Reverend [First Name, Surname], Archbishop of [Location]"
- At the beginning of the letter: "Your Grace" or "Dear Archbishop [Surname]"

Addressing a bishop
In person, he should be addressed as, "My Lord" or "Bishop [Surname]"

On the envelope: In England, Wales and Scotland, "The Right Reverend [First Name, Surname, Bishop of [Location]"
In Ireland, "The Most Reverend [First Name, Surname]"
- At the beginning of the letter: "Dear Bishop [Surname]"

Addressing a vicar general
On the envelope:
In England, Wales and Scotland, "The Reverend Monsignor [First Name, Surname] VG"
In Ireland, "The Right Reverend Monsignor [First Name, Surname] VG"
- At the beginning of the letter: "Dear Monsignor [Surname]"

Addressing the Dean of the Chapter

On the envelope:

In England, Wales and Scotland, "The Reverend Dean [First Name, Surname]" or "Dean"

In Ireland, "The Very Reverend [First Name] Dean [Surname]"

- At the beginning of the letter: "Dear Dean [Surname]"

Addressing an archdeacon

On the envelope: "The Venerable Archdeacon [First Name, Surname]"

- At the beginning of the letter: "Dear Archdeacon [Surname]"

Addressing a canon

On the envelope:

In England, Wales and Scotland, "The Reverend Canon [First Name, Surname]" or "Father"

In Ireland, "The Very Reverend [First Name] Canon [Surname]"

- At the beginning of the letter: "Dear Canon [Surname]"

Addressing a priest

On the envelope:

In England, Wales and Scotland, "The Reverend Father [First Name, Surname]" or "Father"

In Ireland (for a parish priest), "The Very Reverend [First Name, Surname] PP"

- At the beginning of the letter: "Dear Father [Surname]"

Addressing a deacon

On the envelope: "The Reverend Deacon [First Name, Surname]"

- At the beginning of the letter: "Dear Deacon [Surname]"

Addressing a lay chaplain

Simply use their formal name in public and follow the rules of the relevant institution (school, hospital, prison, etc.) for the protocols for addressing staff

Addressing a religious brother/sister

In person, he or she should be addressed as "Brother [First Name]" or "Sister [First Name]"

On the envelope: "Brother [First Name (and Surname if known)], initials of the Religious Order (e.g. OFM)]" or "Sister [First Name (and Surname if known)], initials of the Religious Order (e.g. OFS)]"

- At the beginning of the letter: "Dear Brother [First Name]" or "Dear Sister [First Name]"

* If you are outside of England, Wales, Scotland and Ireland, you should check your local directories.

APPENDIX II
A glossary of Catholic terms

The following list is by no means exhaustive, but it includes many words and phrases you may come across

A

Absolution: part of the sacrament of reconciliation. It is the formal declaration by the priest that a penitent's sins are forgiven.

Abstinence: refraining from certain kinds of food or drink as an act of self-denial. Official days when Catholics abstain from eating meat are Ash Wednesday and Good Friday. In 2011, the Bishops of England and Wales called upon Catholics to re-establish the practice on other Fridays throughout the year, to mark the day on which Jesus died. The Bishops of Ireland also insist on Friday penance (in their 1983 statement), but they leave the form of penance to each person.

Acceptance into the Order of Catechumens: the first liturgical rite, which marks the beginning of the catechumenate proper, as the enquirers express and the Church accepts their intention to respond to God's call to follow the way of Christ – and they become the catechumens.

Advent: the season of the Church's year leading up to Christmas. It includes the four Sundays before Christmas and it is a time of preparation for the coming of Christ. Advent marks the beginning of the Church's year.

All Saints' Day: is the day on which Catholics remember all the saints of the Church, whether officially canonised or not. It is celebrated on 1 November.

All Souls' Day: is the day on which Catholics remember the dead and pray for them, recognising those that may still need to be brought to perfection. It is observed on 2 November and is officially titled the "Commemoration of all the Faithful Departed".

Altar: the table of the Lord, around which the people gather to celebrate the sacrifice of the Mass.

Angel: the word means "messenger". In the Bible, they are described as carrying messages from God to human beings.

Angelus: a form of prayer said three times a day: in the morning, at noon and in the evening. When said in monasteries or churches, it is customary to ring the bells.

Annulment: the declaration by a Church court that a marriage, upon which it had been asked to adjudicate, never existed.

Annunciation: the "announcement" by the angel Gabriel to Mary that she was to be the mother of the Saviour. The feast of the Annunciation is celebrated on 25 March.

Apostolate: the work of an apostle. It is used to describe any work, ministry or service which is carried out on behalf of the Church. For example, the apostolate of a religious order is the work the order undertakes.

Ascension: the taking up of Jesus into heaven forty days after the resurrection and witnessed by the apostles. Ascension Day is celebrated forty days after Easter or on the following Sunday.

Ash Wednesday: the first day of Lent. By tradition, Catholics have ashes put on their foreheads or heads on this day as a mark of repentance. They also fast on this day and abstain from eating meat.

Assumption: the taking up of Mary, the mother of Jesus, into heaven. Catholics celebrate this on 15 August.

Ave Maria: Latin words meaning "Hail Mary", the first words of the most popular prayer Catholics address to Mary.

B

Basilica: a large and significant church. The most famous basilica is St Peter's Basilica in Rome.

Beatification: the first step in the process by which a dead person is officially declared to be a saint.

Benediction: a service in which the consecrated Host is placed in a monstrance where it can be seen and venerated by the people. At the conclusion of the service, the priest blesses the people with the monstrance containing the Host.

Bidding prayers: are the prayers which are said at Mass for the needs of the Church and the world. Also referred to as the **Prayer of the Faithful** or the **general intercessions**. The Church prays not just for its own needs but for the salvation of the world, for civil authorities, for those oppressed by any burden, and for the local community, particularly those who are sick or who have died.

Blessed Sacrament: a term Catholics use when referring to the consecrated Host – especially when it is reserved in the tabernacle.

Blessing: a short prayer, usually accompanied by the sign of the cross, asking God's favour on persons or objects.

Breviary: a book containing the prayers, hymns, psalms and readings which make up the Divine Office - the official prayer of the Church said at various times during the day.

C

Canonisation: the official declaration by the Pope that a dead person is a saint and may be publicly venerated.

Canon Law: the law of the Church.

Catechesi Tradendae: (Latin for "Catechesis in Our Time"), a post-synodal apostolic exhortation of Pope John Paul II, published 16 October 1979, on the topic of catechesis in the contemporary world.

Catechesis: the process of "transmitting the Gospel, as the Christian community has received it, understands it, celebrates it, lives it and communicates it in many ways"(*General Directory for Catechesis* #105). The word catechesis comes from the Greek meaning "to echo the teaching", meaning that catechesis or the teaching of the faith is an interactive process in which the word of God re-sounds between and among the proclaimer, the one receiving the message and the Holy Spirit. (Source: Catholic News Agency.)

Catechesis, General Directory for: see *General Directory for Catechesis*.

Catechism: a written summary of Christian teaching.

Catechist: The role of a catechist is to put people not only in touch but in communion, in intimacy, with Jesus Christ. They catechise people of all ages and abilities both by word and example.

Catechumenate, Period of the: the time for the nurturing and growth of the catechumens' faith and conversion to God. Minor rites included in this period are the celebrations of the word and prayers of exorcism and blessing and are meant to assist the process.

Celebrant: the one who presides at a religious service. The priest at Mass is referred to as the celebrant or presider.

Chalice: the cup used at Mass to hold the wine (the precious Blood).

Chapter: the governing body of a cathedral or other religious community.

Chrism: a mixture of olive oil and balsam which is blessed by the bishop in Holy Week and used in the administration of the sacraments of **baptism**, **confirmation** and **holy orders**, and in the consecration of churches.

Christ the King: now known as Our Lord Jesus Christ, King of the Universe, this feast is celebrated on the last Sunday of the Church's year acclaiming Christ as king of the universe.

Ciborium: a bowl or chalice-shaped vessel to hold the consecrated Hosts for the distribution of **Holy Communion**.

Clergy: a term applied to men who have been ordained for ministry in the Church. Bishops, priests and deacons are members of the clergy.

Communion: see **Holy Communion**.

Communion under both kinds: receiving **Holy Communion** under the forms of bread and wine. It is becoming increasingly common for Catholics to receive Holy Communion this way – particularly on special occasions.

Concelebration: the celebration of Mass by several priests together.

Conclave: the meeting of the cardinals, in complete seclusion, when they assemble to elect a pope.

Confession, sacrament of: the admission of **sins** or faults to a priest (who is acting *in persona Christi*) who gives the sinner **absolution**. See also: **Reconciliation, the sacrament of.**

Confessor: a priest who hears confessions. In the early church, Christians who confessed their faith while suffering persecution were given this title.

Contrition: the acknowledgement of sin and sorrow for it.

Convent: the place where a community of nuns lives.

Corpus Christi: (Latin for "the Body of Christ"). The feast of Corpus Christi commemorates the institution of the Eucharist and is celebrated on the Thursday after Trinity Sunday, or the following Sunday. The feast is sometimes marked by a procession with the Blessed Sacrament.

Creed: a summary of Christian beliefs.

Crucifix: a cross with the figure of the crucified Jesus upon it. Used by Catholics to bring to mind the sufferings, kingship and triumph of Christ.

D

Deanery: several parishes form a deanery, sometimes called a "pastoral area". This unit is administered by one of the priests of the deanery, usually appointed by the bishop.

Devil: the name for the evil one, a creature who rebelled against God and causes evil.

Diocese: an area under the care of a bishop.

Dispensation: exemption from a Church law in a particular case for a special reason.

Doctrines: the beliefs of Catholics expressed in the Creed and other official documents.

Dogma: doctrines put forward by the Church which are to be accepted as true and clear statements of belief.

E

Easter: the day on which Jesus rose from the dead.

Easter Vigil: also called the Paschal Vigil or the Great Vigil of Easter, the Easter Vigil liturgy is the most beautiful liturgy in the Roman Catholic Church, marking the triumph of the Light of Christ over the darkness of death. The dramatic Easter Vigil liturgy, celebrated during the night that precedes Easter Day, marks the beginning of Easter.

Ecumenism: the work for unity between the different Christian Churches.

Election or Enrolment of Names: this is the second liturgical rite of the RCIA, usually celebrated on the First Sunday of Lent, when the Church formally ratifies the catechumens' readiness for the **sacraments of initiation** and the catechumens, who are now the elect, express their desire for the sacraments.

Enclosure: that part of a convent or monastery to which outsiders are not admitted.

Encyclical: a letter from the Pope to the whole Church, usually dealing with matters of faith and the Christian life.

Enquiry Period: a time, of no fixed duration or structure, for enquiry and introduction to Gospel values, an opportunity for the beginnings of faith (also known as Pre-catechumenate or Period of Evangelisation).

Epiphany: the feast which commemorates the visit of the magi to the infant Christ in Bethlehem. It is celebrated on 6 January or on the second Sunday after Christmas.

Evangelisation, Period of: a time, of no fixed duration or structure, for enquiry and introduction to Gospel values for potential RCIA candidates, an opportunity for the beginnings of faith (also known as **Enquiry Period** or **Pre-catechumenate**).

Excommunication: is the cutting off from the community of the Church because of serious offences against its law or teaching. It is resorted to only rarely.

F

Fasting: eating less food than usual as an act of self-denial. Catholics fast especially on Ash Wednesday and Good Friday. Fasting is obligatory from age 18 until age 59. When *fasting*, a person is permitted to eat one full meal.

Feast day: a day of special solemnity within the Church.

First Friday: see **Sacred Heart.** Mass is usually celebrated on First Fridays in most churches, and the sick are brought Communion in their homes.

Font: a basin or bowl in a church used for the baptismal water.

Friday Penance: in commemoration of the sufferings of Christ, Catholics perform some act of self-denial every Friday. This may take the form of abstaining from meat, or some other food, or doing an act of charity.

G

General Directory for Catechesis: is the document that guides the Church on the ministry of faith formation. It originates with the Congregation for Clergy. It succeeds the 1971 *General Catechetical Directory* in 1997. From this ample work, national conferences, bishops, dioceses, parishes and their ministers derive guidance for directing the faith formation of believers.

General intercessions: see **Bidding prayers.** Also known as **Prayer of the Faithful.**

Genuflection: kneeling on one knee as a sign of honour and worship to Jesus Christ and an expression of faith in his presence in the tabernacle in the Eucharist. Catholics genuflect when entering and leaving a church.

Godparent: someone who assists the parents in ensuring that a child who is baptised will be brought up in the Catholic faith. The godparent must be a Catholic though he or she may be assisted by a member of another Christian Church.

Good Friday: is the day on which the crucifixion of Jesus is commemorated. It is a day of special solemnity for Catholics. They fast and abstain from meat on this day.

Gospel: a word meaning "good news". It is the proclamation of the Good News of salvation won for us by Jesus Christ. The word is also used of the four books which tell of the life, death and resurrection of Jesus: the Gospels of Matthew, Mark, Luke and John.

Grace: is the gift of God's love and help which is given to us freely, without any previous efforts on our part.

Grace at meals: a short prayer before and after meals thanking God for the food we eat and asking his blessing on those who have prepared it.

H

Habit: the distinctive form of dress worn by members of religious communities.

Hail Mary: is the most popular prayer Catholics address to our Lady. It derives from the angel's greeting (Luke 1:28) and the greeting of Mary's cousin, Elizabeth (Luke 1:42), adding to these a request for Mary to pray for us.

Heaven: the endless moment of love. Nothing more separates us from God, whom our soul loves and has sought our whole life long.

Hell: the condition of everlasting separation from God, which our freedom makes possible.

Heresy: a teaching that contradicts the beliefs of the Catholic Church.

Holy day of obligation: a solemnity – when the faithful are obliged to participate in the Mass, and to abstain from anything which prevents them from worshipping God. Every Sunday is a holy day of obligation.

Holy Hour: a service in which Jesus is venerated in the Blessed Sacrament.

Holy orders: the sacrament or rite of ordination as a bishop, priest, or deacon. It is the sacrament through which the mission entrusted by Christ to his apostles continues to be exercised in the Church until the end of time: thus it is the sacrament of apostolic ministry. It includes three degrees: episcopate, presbyterate, and diaconate (CCC 1536). See **Ordination.**

Holy Saturday: the day between Good Friday and Easter Sunday.

Holy Thursday (or Maundy Thursday): the day before Good Friday. On this day, Catholics commemorate the supper Jesus had with his disciples on the night before he died.

Holy water: is water that has been blessed by a priest. Catholics bless themselves with holy water as they make the sign of the cross on entering a church as a reminder of their baptism. Holy water is also used for various blessings and at home.

Holy Week: is the final week of Lent, leading up to Easter Sunday. The last three days of Holy Week (Holy Thursday, Good Friday and Holy Saturday) are days of special solemnity.

Homily: see **Sermon.**

Host: is the consecrated Eucharist in the form of bread; the large host is broken by the priest at Mass and small hosts are used to distribute to the people, and to reserve in the tabernacle. Also used casually to mean unconsecrated altar-breads.

I

Icon: the prayed depiction of Christ, Mary, of the saints, painted in the style of the Eastern (Orthodox) Church. Often painted on wood and adorned with precious stones.

Immaculate Conception: the doctrine that Mary was conceived in the womb of her mother, without inheriting original sin (not to be confused with the virgin birth of Jesus, which refers to his birth). Catholics celebrate the Immaculate Conception on 8 December.

Impediment to marriage: is something that prevents a person entering into a Church marriage. For example, certain degrees of blood-relationship between partners, or where one partner is not baptised. A dispensation can be obtained from some impediments.

Incarnation: the mystery of the wonderful union of the divine and human natures in the person of Jesus Christ.

Indulgence: remission of the punishment or penance due to sin after its guilt has been forgiven.

Intercession: the prayers the saints in heaven offer to God on behalf of people on earth who request their help.

J

Jesus: there are a number of symbols for the name Jesus which you may use in churches or in works of religious art. These are some of them:
- *ICHTHYS:* an acrostic consisting of the initial letters of five Greek words forming the word for fish, which represent the divine character of Jesus: Iesous (Jesus), Christos (Christ), Theou (God's), Yios (Son) and Soter (Saviour).
- *INRI:* the initial letters from the Latin inscription written on the cross: "Jesus Nazarenus Rex Iudaeorum" (Jesus of Nazareth, King of the Jews).

- *XP:* a monogram of the first two Greek letters of "Christos".

Joseph: the husband of Mary, venerated as a saint. His feast is celebrated on 19 March.

K

Kyrie, eleison: Greek words meaning "Lord, have mercy". Sometimes said or sung in Greek during the Penitential Rite of the Mass.

L

Laicisation: the process by which a member of the clergy returns to the lay state (does not invalidate his ordination).

Laity: all baptised Christians are members of the laity, sharing the "common priesthood of all the faithful".

Last Judgement: the judgement of every person by Jesus Christ at the end of time.

Last Supper: the supper Jesus had with his disciples on the night before he died, during which he instituted the Eucharist.

Lay: the word lay derives from the Anglo-French *lai* (from Late Latin *laicus*, from the Greek – laikos, of the people; from – *laos*, the people at large).

Lay apostolate: work done by laypeople as a response to their baptismal calling.

Lectern: the stand from which the scriptures are read in church.

Lectio Divina: a reflective reading of the scripture leading to meditation on specific passages (often used by parish groups preparing the following Sunday's scripture readings).

Lectionary: the three-volume book of the Church's scripture readings, used in the Mass and other liturgies.

Lent: is a period of seven weeks leading up to Easter, or six weeks up to Holy Week. It begins on Ash Wednesday and is a time of prayer, fasting and works of love. The traditional purpose of Lent is the preparation of the believer through prayer, penance, repentance of sins, almsgiving, atonement and self-denial for Easter.

Litany: a form of prayer in which the minister recites a series of petitions to God, or calls on the help of the saints. These petitions are followed by a set response said or sung by the congregation.

Liturgical year: the worship of the Church over the period of a year during which the central mysteries of faith are unfolded. The chief festivals are Christmas, Easter and Pentecost.

Liturgy: is the public worship of the Church.

Lord's Prayer: the prayer Jesus taught his followers to say: the Our Father.

M

Magisterium: is the teaching authority of the Church.

Martyr: a Christian who bears witness to the truth of the Gospel to the point of death.

Mass: the Sunday Eucharist is popularly known as the Mass among Catholics, a name derived from the words of dismissal at its end (*Ite, missa est*, meaning: "go, you are dismissed").

Mass intentions, offerings: a priest may offer a Mass for a particular intention (e.g. for the healing of someone who is sick or for the eternal salvation of someone who has died). He will usually receive a cash donation for this, called a "Mass offering" also known as a **stipend**. The Bishops' Conference usually specify how much this should be.

Maundy Thursday: see **Holy Thursday.**

May devotions: are special services held during the month of May to honour Mary, the mother of Jesus.

Meditation: reflecting on God, the word of God or on the things of God in one's heart.

Missal: a book containing the prayers of the Mass.

Missionaries: Christians who proclaim the Gospel to others, anyone who endeavours to share his or her faith with others. To be a Christian is to be a missionary.

Mixed marriage: a marriage between a Catholic and a person of a different faith. Catholics need permission from the Church before they can contract such a marriage.

Monstrance: a (sometimes) ornate receptacle in which a consecrated Host is placed so that Jesus, in the Host, can be seen and venerated by the people.

Mortal (or serious) sin: is a grave sin in the knowing and wilful violation of God's law in a serious matter, for example, idolatry, adultery, murder, slander. Catholics who are conscious of having committed a mortal sin are bound to confess to a priest. Three conditions are necessary for a mortal sin to exist: the matter must be grave (or immoral); the person must know that what they are doing is evil and immoral and the person must freely choose to commit the act (CCC 1857).

Mother of God: a title given to Mary because she is the mother of Jesus who is both God and man.

Mystagogy: also known as the Period of Post-baptismal Catechesis. See **Post-baptismal Catechesis, Period of.**

Mystery: a truth which cannot be grasped by human reason.

N

New Testament: is made up of twenty-seven different books attributed to eight different authors, six of whom are numbered among the apostles (Matthew, John, Paul, James, Peter, Jude) and two among their immediate disciples (Mark, Luke). The New Testament was not written all at once. The books that compose it appeared one after another in the space of 200-250 years. The New Testament discusses the teachings and person of Jesus, as well as events in first-century Christianity.

Novena: nine days of devotions, containing a daily Mass or Rosary or other prayers.

Nuptial Mass: a Mass which includes the wedding service. Not all weddings in the Catholic Church are celebrated within Mass. It is quite common to have the wedding service alone (especially when a Catholic is marrying a non-Catholic).

O

Old Testament: the Hebrew scriptures that were composed before the time of Christ. They bring the revelation of God's covenant in which he would call a people to himself and be their God. This understanding of a people united in a covenant or testament, carries forward into the New Testament as it unfolds in the life of Jesus and the creation of the Church.

Ordinary (The): bishop or major religious superior, to whom priests in his diocese or community make vows of obedience.

Ordinariate: The Personal Ordinariate of Our Lady of Walsingham was established by Pope Benedict XVI to allow Anglicans to enter into the full communion of the Catholic Church while retaining much of their heritage and traditions.

Ordination: the conferring of holy orders on a man, by which he becomes a bishop, priest or deacon.

Ordo: the Liturgical Calendar.

Our Lady: the title Catholics most frequently use when referring to Mary, the mother of Jesus.

ρ

Pagan: a collective term meaning "unbelievers".

Palm Sunday: the Sunday before Easter. It commemorates the occasion when Jesus rode into Jerusalem on a donkey and the people waved palm branches in his honour. In the Catholic Church, this Sunday is now called Palm Sunday of the Passion of the Lord.

Parables: the stories Jesus told which illustrate some of his most important teachings.

Paradise: another word for heaven. It is also used of the Garden of Eden.

Parish: the community of the Church in a particular place. In Latin, the word *parocoeia*, a Latinised version of the Greek word παροικία, originally referred to neighbours or people living near each other.

Parish pastoral council (PPC): a group of people of a parish who, together with the parish priest, look after the pastoral needs of the parish.

Parish mission: a period of spiritual renewal within a parish, usually conducted by one or more visiting priests over a period of a week or a fortnight.

Passion: the suffering and death of Jesus on the cross.

Passion Sunday: see **Palm Sunday.**

Pastoral care: the caring work of the Church. The word pastoral comes from "pastor" meaning "shepherd".

Pastoral letter: a letter sent from a bishop to his diocese on a number of occasions during the year. Pastoral letters are usually read out to the people during the Mass.

Pax Christi: literally, "the peace of Christ". It is the name of an international Catholic movement for Justice and Peace.

Penance: refers to the sacrament of penance, **confession** or the sacrament of **reconciliation** (which is more often used now). The word "penance" also refers to acts of self-denial. For example, fasting can be described as an act of penance. See also **Reconciliation, the sacrament of.**

Pentecost: literally means "fiftieth day". It marks the day when the Holy Spirit came upon the apostles fifty days after the resurrection of Jesus. It is also called Whit Sunday.

Petition: is a prayer asking God for our needs.

Pilgrimage: a journey to a holy place. Popular places of pilgrimage today include the Holy Land, Rome, Walsingham, Knock and Lourdes.

Post-baptismal Catechesis, Period of: this is the time, usually the Easter season, following the celebration of initiation, during which the newly initiated experience being fully part of the Christian community by means of pertinent catechesis and particularly by participation with all the faithful in the Sunday Eucharistic celebration. This leads to the rest of their lives lived in faith, hope and charity (also known as **Mystagogy**).

Postulant: a person who has applied to join a religious order and is waiting to be admitted. They can also be called "candidate" or "aspirant".

Prayer of the Faithful: see **Bidding prayers**.

Preaching: at his **ordination** the priest promises to celebrate the mysteries of Christ faithfully and religiously, as the Church has handed them down to us for the glory of God and the sanctification of Christ's people, and to exercise the ministry of the Word worthily and wisely, preaching the Gospel and explaining the Catholic faith (CTM 37).

Pre-catechumenate: a time, of no fixed duration or structure, for enquiry and introduction to Gospel values, an opportunity for the beginnings of faith (also known as **Enquiry Period** or Period of Evangelisation).

Preface: the first part of the Eucharistic Prayer in the Mass.

Presbytery: the house, often adjoining the church, where the priest of the parish lives.

Procession: a solemn walk for a religious purpose, usually accompanied by prayers and hymns. Processions are not as commonplace nowadays as they once were; but they are still held occasionally. For example, **Palm Sunday**, the May processions in honour of our Lady or processions for **Corpus Christi.**

Profession: the taking of vows on joining a religious order.

Purgatory: a state in which the souls of the dead are purified and perfected in love before finally becoming one with God in heaven.

Purification and Enlightenment, Period of: usually the Lenten season preceding the celebration of initiation at the Easter Vigil; it is a time of reflection, centred on conversion, marked by celebration of the scrutinies and presentations and of the preparation rites on Holy Saturday.

R

Readers: those who read the scripture passages during Mass. Passages from the Old Testament or parts of the New Testament may be read by laypeople (men and women). Passages from the Gospels are always read by a priest or a deacon.

Real Presence: the phrase Catholics use to indicate their belief that the bread and wine offered during the Mass become the Body and Blood of Christ.

Reconciliation, the sacrament of: imparts to the sinner the love of God. It is also called the sacrament of conversion, the sacrament of **penance**, the sacrament of **confession** and the sacrament of forgiveness (CCC 1423–1424).

Redemption: being delivered from evil through the birth, life, death and resurrection of Jesus Christ.

Reformation: a movement for the reform of certain doctrines and practices of the Church which began in the sixteenth century and led to the division between the Catholic and Protestant (or Reformed) Churches.

Religious order: the name given to a community of men or women dedicated to some specific mission. See **Vows**.

Requiem: a Mass for the dead. It takes its name from the first word of the prayer with which the Mass begins. In Latin, this is *"Requiem aeternam dona eis, Domine"* (Lord, give them eternal rest).

Responsorial psalm: a psalm which is recited or sung after the first scripture reading at Mass. The congregation recites or sings a response after each verse.

Resurrection of the body: the doctrine that, at the end of time, all will rise – body and soul – from the dead and live with God for ever or be condemned.

Revelation: God's disclosure of himself to humanity. The greatest revelation of God is Jesus Christ.

Rosary: a form of prayer reflecting on the main events in the life of Jesus and Mary, his mother. There are twenty of these events, called "mysteries", divided into four groups: Joyful, Luminous, Sorrowful and Glorious. The prayers which go with each mystery are: one Our Father, ten Hail Marys, one Glory be to the Father. Rosary beads are used to help count the prayers. The repetition of the prayer is an aid to concentration.

S

Sacrament: a rite or ceremony which imparts divine grace. In the Catholic Church, there are seven sacraments: baptism, confirmation, the Eucharist, reconciliation (also known as penance or confession), marriage, holy orders and anointing the sick (which used to be called Extreme Unction or the Last Rites).

Sacraments of Initiation, Celebration of the: this is the third liturgical rite, usually integrated into the Easter Vigil by which the elect are initiated through baptism, confirmation, and the Eucharist.

Sacramentals: rites, objects or actions intended to aid devotion which have some resemblance to sacraments. An example of a sacramental is the use of holy water.

Sacred Heart: the heart of Jesus is honoured as a sign of his love for all people. The feast of the Most Sacred Heart of Jesus is celebrated in June and there is a tradition among many Catholics of honouring Jesus under this title on the first Friday of every month.

Sacristy: the room in the church where the priest vests for Mass and other services and where the sacred vessels are kept.

Saints: members of the Church whose holiness of life is recognised after their death and who are venerated by the Church on earth. Before anyone can be proclaimed a saint (canonised), a process of careful investigation of their life is carried out.

Sanctuary: the area around the altar is called the sanctuary; it is also considered holy because of the physical presence of God in the Eucharist, both during the Mass on the altar and in the tabernacle the rest of the time.

Sanctuary lamp: a lamp which is kept burning near the tabernacle in Catholic churches as a sign and a reminder that Jesus is present in the Blessed Sacrament.

Seminary: a college where men are trained for the priesthood.

Serious sin: see **Mortal sin**.

Sign of the cross: a formula Catholics use to bless themselves. It is made with the right hand by touching the forehead, the breast and the shoulders while saying the words: "In the name of the Father, and of the Son and of the Holy Spirit. Amen." Catholics make the sign of the cross at the beginning of Mass, at the beginning of other forms of prayer and sometimes when beginning an activity or at the start of a new day.

Sin: a rejection of God, usually through action or inaction, for example, when a person acts in a way which is not loving – or does not act as a loving person when they know they should.

Sin, venial: a person commits a venial sin in two cases: when s/he does not observe God's law in a less serious matter or when s/he did not have full knowledge or give full consent in a grave matter. Venial sins show disordered affections and impede the person's progress in virtue (CCC 1862–1863).

Society of St Vincent de Paul (SVP): a society of men and women willing to undertake active charitable works.

Soul: the spiritual element of a person's nature.

Stations of the Cross: a series of fourteen meditations on incidents from the suffering and death of Christ. Images of these fourteen scenes can be found around Catholic churches. There is sometimes a fifteenth one, "the resurrection".

Stipend: see **Mass intentions, offerings.**

SVP: see **Society of St Vincent de Paul**.

Synod: a Church council, for example the synod of bishops which is held in Rome at roughly three-year intervals and is attended by about 200 bishops from all over the world.

T

Tabernacle: usually an ornate box where the **Blessed Sacrament** is reserved.

Ten Commandments: the rules of life delivered by God to Moses on Mount Sinai. They still form the basis of morality for Christians and Jews.

Theology: articulating and exploring our experience of God, who reveals himself to us.

Tradition: the teaching which has been handed down from the apostles of Jesus and which continues to be handed on by the Church in every age.

Transubstantiation: a word Catholics use to describe the way in which Jesus becomes present in the Eucharistic bread and wine.

Triduum: The Easter Triduum is the three-day period which forms the climax of the liturgical year. It runs from sunset on Holy Thursday to sunset on Easter Sunday. Other three-day periods of prayer or devotions are also called by the name "triduum".

Trinity Sunday: the Sunday after Pentecost. It is a day on which even more special honour is paid to the Blessed Trinity.

V

Vatican: a sovereign city state and the official residence of the Pope in Rome. It also refers to the central governance of the Church.

Venial sin: see **Sin, venial**.

Vestments: garments worn by the ministers of the Church when celebrating Mass or administering the sacraments. These include the *alb* – a long tunic worn by all ministers; the *chasuble* – the main outer garment of the priest when celebrating the Mass; the *stole* – a type of scarf worn around the neck. The stole is worn by all clergy when administering the sacraments.

Viaticum: Holy Communion given to a person who is dying. The word means "provision for a journey", namely the journey through death to life in the world to come.

Virgin birth: the doctrine that Mary remained a virgin before, during and after the birth of Jesus, her son. This doctrine preserves the truth that Jesus was both God and man. He was "conceived by the Holy Spirit", meaning that his origin is wholly from God; he was "born of the Virgin Mary" meaning that he is fully human.

Vocation: the calling to a life of love, service and holiness which is addressed to all people. This may be a calling to the priesthood or religious life; it may be a calling to the married life or single life.

Vows: solemn promises which are made by a couple when they marry; and by members of religious orders, who often promise poverty, chastity and obedience to God. In the case of religious vows, they can be temporary (binding only for a time) or perpetual (binding for life).

W

Whit Sunday: another name for the feast of Pentecost which celebrates the Holy Spirit coming upon the apostles. "Whit" means "white". In earlier times, the newly baptised wore the white robes of baptism on this day.

APPENDIX III
Useful reference materials and websites

Further reading

Bausch, William J., *The Parish of the Next Millennium* (Twenty-Third Publications, Mystic, CT, 1997).

Carr, W., *Brief Encounters: Pastoral Ministry through Baptisms, Weddings and Funerals* (SPCK, London, 1994).

Delaney, Martin and Maeve Mahon, *Do This in Memory of Me* (Veritas, Dublin, 2006).

Doherty, Tony, *So you're Working for the Catholic Church: a friendly guide to the Catholic Tradition* (Paulist Press International, US, 2010).

Dunning, James, *Echoing God's War* (American Forum on the Catechumenate, Arlington, 1993).

Dunning, James, *New Wine: New Wineskins, Pastoral Implications of the Rite of Christian Initiation of Adults* (William Sadler, Chicago, New York, Los Angeles, 1981).

Groome, Thomas, *Christian Religious Education – Sharing Our Story and Vision* (Harper Collins Publishers, New York, 1980).

Groome, Thomas, *What makes us Catholic?* (Harper Collins Publishers, New York, 2003).

Gula, Richard M., SS, *Just Ministry – Professional Ethics for Pastoral Ministers* (Paulist Press, New York/Mahwah New Jersey, 2010).

Guzie, Tad, *The Book of Sacramental Basics* (Paulist Press, New York, Mahwah, 1981).

Hayes, Michael A. and Liam Gearon (eds.), *Contemporary Catholic Theology: A Reader* (Gracewing Publishing, London, 1998).

Jarema, William J., *A Survival Guide for Church Ministers*, (Paulist Press US, 2011).

Klein, Diana, *Symbols of faith – faith formation and sacramental preparation for people with learning disabilities* (Redemptorist Publications, Chawton, 2015).

Klein, Diana and Susanne Kowal, (members of the CICCA Working Party of the Bishops' Conference of England and Wales), *I Call You Friends: Book 3* (McCrimmons, Great Wakering, Essex, 2009).

This book is part of Living and Sharing Our Faith: A National Project for Catechesis and Religious Education.

Klein, Diana, *The Christ we proclaim – Christian Initiation of Children of Catechetical Age* (an online publication of Westminster Diocese, London, 2010). For access: http://issuu.com/exploringfaith/docs/cicca_catechistsbook http://issuu.com/exploringfaith/docs/cicca_childrensbook.

O'Leary, Daniel, *Begin with the Heart: Recovering a Sacramental Imagination* (Columbia Press, Blackrock, 2008).

Ratcliffe, Timothy, OP, *What's the point of being a Christian?* (Burns & Oates, London, 2005).

Rohr, Richard, OFM, *Things Hidden: Scripture as spirituality* (St Anthony Messenger Press, Cincinnati, 2008).

Schreck, A., *The Compact History of the Catholic Church* (Servant Books, Cincinnati, 2009).

Scott, Peter Michael, *My Hospital Prayer & Activities book* (Redemptorist Publications, Chawton, 2014).

Sofield, Loughlan and Carroll Juliano, *Collaborative Ministry* (Ave Maria Press, Notre Dame, Indiana, 1995).

Towey, Anthony, *Introduction to Christian Theology* (Bloomsbury T&T Clark, London, 2013).

Church documents

Vatican II documents (which you will find on www.vatican.va):

Focus on spirituality:
- *Sacrosanctum Concilium* (The Constitution on the Sacred Liturgy)
- *Dei Verbum* (Decree on Divine Revelation)

Focus on the Church:
- *Lumen Gentium* (Dogmatic Constitution on the Church)
- *Christus Dominus* (Decree concerning the Pastoral Office of Bishops in the Church)
- *Optatam Totius* (Decree on Priestly Formation)

- *Apostolicam Actuositatem* (Decree on the Apostolate of the Laity)
- *Perfectae Caritatis* (Decree on the Sensitive Renewal of Religious Life)
- *Presbyterorum Ordinis* (Decree on the Ministry and Life of Priests)
- *Ad Gentes* (Decree on the Church's Missionary Activity)

Focus on the Church in the world of today:
- *Gaudium et Spes* (Pastoral Constitution on the Church in the Modern World)

Encyclicals (which you will find on www.vatican.va):

- *Laudato Si'* (Encyclical Letter on the care of our common home) – Pope Francis, 2015
- *Evangelii Gaudium* (The Joy of the Gospel) – Pope Francis, 2013
- *Lumen Fidei* (The Light of Faith) – Pope Francis, 2013
- *Caritas in Veritate* (Charity in Truth) – Pope Benedict XVI, 2009
- *Sacramentum Caritatis* (Apostolic Exhortation on the Eucharist) – Pope Benedict XVI, 2007
- *Deus Caritas Est* (God is Love) – Pope Benedict XVI, 2005
- *Fides et Ratio* (Faith and Reason) – Pope John Paul II, 1995
- *Evangelium Vitae* (The Gospel of Life) – Pope John Paul II, 1995
- *Centesimus Annus* (The Hundredth Year) – Pope John Paul II, 1991
- *Sollicitudo Rei Socialis* (On Social Concern) – Pope John Paul II, 1987
- *Laborem Exercens* (On Human Work) – Pope John Paul II, 1981
- *Catechesi Tradendae* (Catechesis in our Time) – Pope John Paul II, 1979
- *Evangelii Nuntiandi* (On Evangelisation in the Modern World) – Pope Paul VI, 1975
- *Justicia in Mundo* (Justice in the World) – Synod of Bishops, 1971
- *Octogesima Adveniens* (A Call to Action) – Pope Paul VI, 1971
- *Populorum Progressio* (On the Development of Peoples) – Pope Paul VI, 1967
- *Pacem in Terris* (Peace on Earth) – Pope John XXIII, 1963
- *Mater et Magistra* (Christianity and Social Progress) – Pope John XXIII, 1961
- *Quadragesimo Anno* (After Forty Years) – Pope Pius XI, 1931
- *Rerum Novarum* (On the Condition of Labour) – Pope Leo XIII, 1891

The Rites (which you can find on www.liturgyoffice.org.uk/Resources/Rites/):

- *The Roman Missal*, International Committee on English in the Liturgy, 2011
- *The Rite of Christian Initiation of Adults*, which includes (as Part II) the *Christian Initiation of Children of Catechetical Age*, The Office of the Sacred Congregation for Divine Worship, 1987
- *The Rite of Baptism for Children*, The Office of the Sacred Congregation for Divine Worship, 1970
- *The Rite of Confirmation*, The Office of the Sacred Congregation for Divine Worship, 1971
- *The Rite of Marriage*, International Committee on English in the Liturgy, 1969
- *The Order of Christian Funerals*, International Committee on English in the Liturgy, 1988

Other Church documents (which you will find on www.vatican.va):

- *Catechism of the Catholic Church* (Geoffrey Chapman, London, 1994).
- *Code of Canon Law* (Collins Liturgical Publications, London, 1983).
- *General Directory of Catechesis*, Congregation for the Clergy, (Catholic Truth Society, London, 1997).

Catholic Bishops' Conference of England and Wales – resources (www.liturgyoffice.org.uk/Resources/):

- *Celebrating the Mass* (CTM) (Catholic Truth Society, London, 2005) is a pastoral guide, a companion and guide to the *General Instruction of the Roman Missal* (GIRM) (Catholic Truth Society, London, 2012), prepared by the Bishops of England and Wales.
- *The Sign We Give*, a report from the Working Party on Collaborative Ministry, (Matthew James Publishing, Ltd., Essex, 1995) (A summary can be found in *The Tablet* archives: http://archive.thetablet.co.uk/article/16th-september-1995/36/the-sign-we-give/).

US Conference of Catholic Bishops (USCCB)

- *Called and Gifted* (1980), *Called and Gifted for the Third Millennium* (1995), on the laity and clergy working together.
- *Co-workers in the Vineyard of the Lord* (2005), a Resource for Guiding the Development of Lay Ecclesial Ministry.
- *National Directory for Catechesis* (2005).

Websites

Vatican website for all the Vatican II documents and encyclicals
- www.vatican.va

Conferences of Bishops:
- **www.bcos.org.uk** Catholic Bishops' Conference of Scotland **www.catholicbishops.ie** Irish Catholic Bishops' Conference
- **www.cbcew.org.uk** Official website of the Catholic Church for England and Wales
- **www.usccb.org** Official website of the US Conference of Catholic Bishops

Aid agencies
- **www.cafod.org.uk** and **www.caritas.eu/country/ englandandwales** CAFOD is the official aid agency of the Catholic Church in England and Wales and part of Caritas International
- **www.trocaire.org** Trócaire is the Irish Charity working for a just world
- **www.sciaf.org.uk** SCIAF is the Scottish Catholic International Aid Fund, the official aid and international development charity of the Catholic Church in Scotland
- **Pontifical Mission Societies** the Pope's official aid agency worldwide. **www.missio.org.uk** (UK); **www.wmi.ie** (Ireland)

Justice and Peace
- **www.justice-and-peace.org.uk** The National Justice and Peace Network links people who have a concern for justice and peace in the UK
- **www.catholicbishops.ie/justice** Council for Justice and Peace of the Irish Catholic Bishops' Conference. This Council comes under the Episcopal Commission for Social Issues and International Affairs
- **www.justiceandpeacescotland.org.uk** The National Commission for Justice and Peace advises the Scottish Bishops' Conference of the Catholic Church in matters relating to social justice

Liturgy
- **www.liturgyoffice.org.uk** The Liturgy Office for the Department for Christian Life and Worship of the Catholic Bishops' Conference of England and Wales
- **www.liturgy-ireland.ie/** The National Centre for Liturgy in Ireland
- **www.scmo.org.uk/bishops_conference/commissions/ liturgy** Liturgy Commission for Scotland

Prayer
- **www.sacredspace.ie** Daily prayers run by the Irish Jesuits

The Tablet
- **www.thetablet.co.uk** *The Tablet* in the weekly Catholic international newspaper – worth a subscription (especially for the Parish Practice page)

Returning Catholics
- **www.CatholicsComeHome.org** Catholics Come Home
- **www.landingsintl.org/returning-to-the-church** Landings International
- **www.kit4catholics.org.uk** Keeping in Touch
- **www.catholicsreturninghome.org** Catholics returning home

INDEX